HABITS THAT WORK

Simple Habits for Radical Results

ONYANGO OWOR

Habits at Work

Simple Habits for Radical Results

onyango@onyangoowor.com
+256 787 367 458

ISBN : 978 -9913-623-09-4

Design and Layout by **Nomad Advertising Ltd**

Dedication

To the curious, ambitious and all those that have longed to ditch their bad habits but didn't know how, why, and when to do so.

TABLE OF CONTENTS

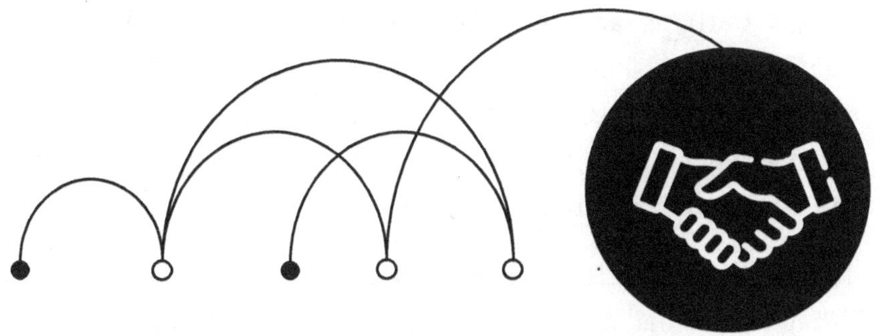

Introduction

Success in any venture or cause has never been by accident. It is a product of sustained intentional effort by the individual. Our present situation or station in life is a result of our habits. Whether we are consciously aware of them or not. Habits shape the kind of person we are becoming or have become, the kind of impact we are having in the world, and the quality of life that we are experiencing.

A habit is defined as an acquired mode of behavior that has become nearly or completely involuntary. The Oxford dictionary defines it as a settled or regular tendency or practice, especially one that is hard to give up, while the Merriam-Webster dictionary defines it as a behavior pattern acquired by frequent repetition or physiologic exposure.

Habits, perhaps, are the greatest power we have to determine our destiny to success, to prosperity, a healthy lifestyle, and fulfillment of our capacities in life. However few people have given attention to the subject of habits and how they influence the quality of their lives.

Take a pause and think for a minute:
What couple had a blissful relationship without habits?

Which people created their wealth without habits?

What genius student excelled without habits?

What sportsperson scaled the heights of notoriety without habits?

What well-paid keynote speaker excelled in their craft without habits?

The list is endless: musician, scientist, teacher, banker, leader, lawyer, and professor etcetera.

In this book, we look at habits with a different approach from other resources. I envisage that it is important to know why, what, and where, before you can fully engage the "how" and the "doing". I have clustered some of the most important habits you need to install in your life into four categories.

Spirit or "Being" habits form the foundation of our existence in life. When we, later on, select specific habits to install in our lives, they must be congruent with who we are, what we want to achieve and what we are passionate about.

Mind habits are about calibrating our minds for high-end productivity. Still, these habits dovetail into being habits to water our daily activities.

Action habits are the things we do. Humans, I perceive, have no problem acting. The problem is taking informed and inspired action. It is important to highlight some crucial action habits that we need to inculcate in our lives.

Finally, **people habits** are a must-have. We are social animals. We could fail miserably in our pursuits because we have not mastered relational habits that are critical to fulfilling our missions in life.

The idea of this book is to do two major things: first, I want to bring to your attention critical habits that we need to know and install in our lives in order to succeed. Second, I want to highlight the importance of intentionality in choosing and installing useful habits in one's life.

There might be a need to uninstall some bad habits that we have that are eating us up automatically and chronically.

This is therefore an action book. It is deliberately designed to help you act. The desired action is for one to recognize, purposely and consciously install good, useful, positive, and impactful habits in their lives.

I wish you a happy and inspired reading.

— PART 1 —

Spirit/Being Habits

To what length would you go to save your own life? Nobody really would know until such a time that their dear lives are at stake. It is at the time that our life is on the edge, and we are in a life-threatening situation, that we would realize what we are *capable of doing* to preserve it.

Amazingly, it is at such a moment that matters related to our spirit take prominence. Our priorities shift and reveal what really matters to us. As such, a crisis has a way of telling us what we should have been focusing on in the first place. For instance, when your loved one is sick and cannot talk to you, that's when you realize how much time you wasted not having a meaningful relationship.

Such revelation of what matters to us, if left on the crisis to be unearthed, will only happen once in a blue moon. If there is no crisis, many of us will never have the benefit of accessing what matters to us.

At the end of the day, matters pertaining to the spirit are the most significant. Unfortunately, we only give "airtime" to spiritual life either in the time of a crisis or towards the end of our lives. However, life itself is about spirit.

Think of any 'successful" entity in the world or even just around you. Find out why they do what they do. You will find that if you removed the spirit out of their being and pursuits, they would come crumbling down. Life is spirit.

What Apple Inc. does today with electronic devices is connected to the "spirit of Apple." If you took a little time to study their vision and mission statements, you will understand why they have some unique habits in their business processes. They don't sell Apple products, they sell "the Spirit of Apple." If you were to nip that spirit in the bud, Apple would come down crumbling.

In the United States, I frequently encountered individuals who spoke very passionately about the "American way of life" and "American exceptionalism." My Chinese friends speak fondly about the "Chinese way of thinking."

Also, think about the orderliness and sense of individual responsibility in Nordic countries. Such thoughtfulness is a result of the collective consciousness of the majority of citizens in these countries over time - the spirit. Remove this spirit and all these countries will become ordinary, disorganized, and poor.

Our biggest mistake in life is that we are oblivious of the spirit. Therefore, we do not pay attention to and take care of habits connected to beefing up our spirit. It reminds us of John Elliot and what is called "the beautiful death."

The man huddled on the cabin floor was slowly freezing to death. It was high in the Rockies in south-western Alberta, and outside a blizzard raged. John Elliot had logged miles that day through the deep snows of the mountain passes. As he checked for avalanches, and as dusk and exhaustion overcame him, he had decided to "hole up." He made it wearily to his cabin but somewhat dazed with fatigue, he did not light a fire or remove his wet clothing.

As the blizzard blasted through the cracks in the old cabin walls, the sleeping forest ranger sank into oblivion, paralyzed by the pleasure of the storm's icy caress. Suddenly, however, his dog sprang into action, and with unrelenting whines, finally managed to rouse his near-comatose friend.

The dog was John's constant companion, a St. Bernard, one of a long line of dogs, famous for their heroics in times of crisis. 'If that dog had not been with me, I would be dead today,' John Elliott says. 'When you are freezing to death you actually feel warm all over, and do not wake up because it feels too good.' [1]

What a profound statement to make. Sometimes, we do not wake up from our ways of doing life to check our spirit because it feels good and yet we are dying. It is important to create spirit habits that will help us form the foundation of our pursuits. The following habits, when practiced, will be helpful in accomplishing this goal.

1 Rick Meyers, E-Sword 2000+ Illustrations for preaching

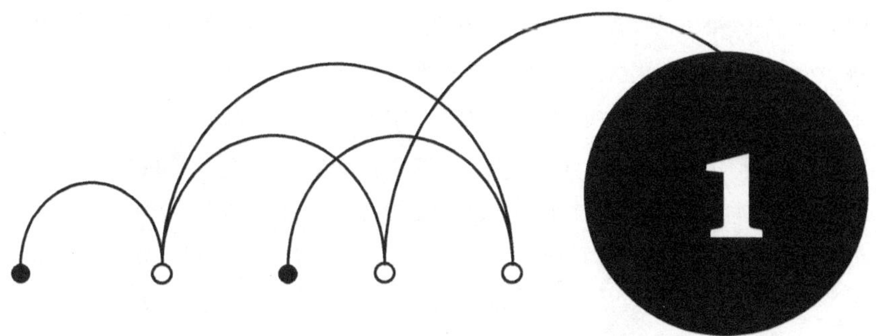

Habit 1: Seeking Clarity

A lot has been spoken about the times and life of Nelson Mandela. Let us take a closer look at one of the most critical moments of his life, the trial at Rivonia. Mandela had been arrested and there was enough evidence against him for the charges of treason. He knew that he needed to be defended, but he decided to take the stand and instead issue a statement. To him, the trial was already a foregone conclusion.

As his life stood in the balance, the very possibility of being sentenced to death hung ominously in the air. Mandela started explaining himself, and I will quote the relevant part in his famous speech that day in 1964.

Our struggle is truly a national one. It is a struggle of the African people inspired by our own suffering and our own experience. It is a struggle for the right to live. During my lifetime, I have dedicated my life to this struggle of the African people. I have fought against white domination, and I have fought against black domination. I have cherished the ideal of a democratic and free society in which all persons will live together in harmony and with equal opportunities. It is an ideal for which I hope to live for and to see realized.

Nelson Mandela was sentenced to life in prison. He was so clear about the cause he wanted his life to take that he was willing to die for it. Obviously, if you read his story, you will notice that it took quite a while for him to come to this clarity. He reminds me of a very high standard that Dr Martin Luther King Jnr speaks of:

'If a man hasn't found something he will die for, he isn't fit to live.'

Therefore, finding clarity about what we want to do with our lives is the most important responsibility we have when we become adults.

If you examine the average person, whether they are employed or not, you will find that a large percentage of them lack clarity in their life's pursuits. If we are to live successful and fulfilling lives, the first habit that we would have would be about clarity of what matters in life.

When we live our lives as if the answers are already available by the time we were born, we miss a great deal of adventure in finding out more about us. Interestingly, we have lots of information on very complex and intricate things in life. However, we lack information about ourselves. We lack clarity about who we are and what matters to us and the role we are intended to play in life.

Many of us have not discovered what *blessing* we should bring to the world. The majority of human beings live by imitation. This includes lawyers and judges who recite jargon and maxims, clad in wigs and robes whose origin they do not know and whose purposes have long lost relevance. If you can imagine with me for a minute, our lives tend to go this way.

One day, a calf walked home through the forest and created a trail. However, this trail was curved, crooked, and skewed. Since then, more than three centuries have passed. The calf is long since dead, but the trail was well marked because it was taken up by a lone dog that went that way too. Then a sheep pursued the trail too and this became a path. Then many men followed the well-trodden path and as they did, they cursed all its crookedness. With us, the path became a lane and then a road that horse carriages followed.

With time, the road became a village street and a city's crowded thoroughfare. It was soon the central street of a renowned metropolis. Three centuries down the road, men have trodden the footsteps of the calf.

Each day a hundred thousand routs followed this zigzag calf about, and over his crooked journey went the traffic of a continent.

A hundred thousand men were thus led by this one calf, three centuries dead. They lost 100 years a day as they followed this crooked way. And thus, men are prone to go it blind along the path of the calf and work from sunrise to sunset to do what other men have done. They follow the hard-beaten path and pursue the dubious course to keep the path that others do.

In fact, they keep the path a sacred edifice, along which all their lives revolve. The wise old woods laugh at them because they saw the calf making the maiden trip back home. [2]

Could it be that what we are doing today is a rote behavior mimicking a "medieval" calf? Humans tend to move in groups, trends, cultures, and dispensations. That way, we easily meet our "belonging" needs. However, this can easily come with a heavy price to pay — lack of personal clarity on what matters in an individual's life.

Every human being has the capacity to achieve clarity in their lives.

Clarity questions

Generally, we need to clarify the following things in our lives:

- Who am I?
- What have I been equipped to do?
- What's the best possible outcome of my life?

---

2. Rick Meyers, E-Sword 2000+ Illustrations for preaching

- Whose pain have I been sent to alleviate?
- What matters to me the most right now?
- What are the most important values that are non-negotiable in my life?
- What are the top 10% activities that I need to engage myself in, in order to churn out the most effectiveness in my life?
- What level of urgency do I need in my life's pursuits?
- What new skills and tools do I need to achieve my life's purpose?
- What are the biggest distractions in my life?
- In what ways am I sabotaging myself?

In order to create the habit of seeking clarity, we need to deploy different tools for different reasons. There are tools for discovery, capture, innovation, and for tracking the clarity that we seek.

Figure 1: Seeking Clarity

Discovery: It is wisdom for focused persons to seek clarity on matters related to their values, vision, mission, and purpose in life. Clarity is needed in the area of the general direction of an individual's life. Your general life mission might not change that often. The same can be said about your purpose.

Seeking clarification about this should be one of the most enlightened things we need to do before we set on our paths of life. To discover your purpose, you will need the following:

Questions: It is popularly said that "questions are answers". You don't know your purpose probably because you haven't been asking, seeking, "knocking on doors for it." Ask empowering questions such as, 'What do I need to do to be more successful and effective?

How can I be of service to other people? What tools do I need to be the best possible version of myself?' Avoid disempowering questions such as, 'Why am I cursed? Why doesn't everything I do succeed?'

Curiosity: This tool will help us question the status quo so that the truth can be revealed. You will easily find that the stumbling block to clarity is status quo.

Purpose quest: You need to go on a journey of discovery of your purpose in life. There are many books that can help you to discover your purpose as well as purpose coaches and mentors.

Capture: There are radio waves all around us. Without a gadget that you can use to capture these waves, you would wrongly assume that the waves do not exist.

In the same way, there is a lot of continuous clarity that comes into our lives daily. That clarity varies from person to person, depending on their passion, quest, cause, capacity, exposure, and interest. You need to tap into these "radio waves" through prayer, quiet time, and meditation.

Alertness: This is a habit that anticipates. When you are in the mode of expectancy, you see a lot of clarity coming into your life. Without alertness, it is not possible to capture the "radio waves around you." Our alertness is the gadget through which we capture waves of clarity about our lives. This is continuous. It never stops. Even an eighty-year-old has clarity coming to their lives.

Intuition: At times, we get a lot of "intelligence" from our intuition. A good habit here would be not only to hone the skills to listen to our intuition, but also to learn to give more trust to it. At times, the most critical information is derived from our intuition and instinct.

In his book, Instinct, TD Jakes shares a powerful story comparing the instinct of a veteran animal tracker to the knowledge of a degree holder in zoology. The veteran was able to help them track an elephant when the professional couldn't. There is so much clarity in your instinct and intuition.

Ideas: Daily, there are powerful ideas that flow through our minds. I envisage that if all of us stopped the traffic and just leaned onto an idea to its logical conclusion, we would not only serve our purpose in life, but we would also transform other people's lives considerably.

Ideas are messages from the divine, infinite intelligence, or life force telling us that we have been entrusted with something new to birth it on the earth. There is not a successful organization in the history of humanity that did not begin with an idea.

Tracking: It is recorded that Socrates, while at his trial, said, 'an unexamined life is not worth living.' There is nothing to add to that. Examine your life regularly. Is it the one you desired and dreamed of? Are you content and fulfilled thus far with your life? Have you discovered your purpose? You can never install a habit consciously without having to track their inspired actions. In order to install the habit of seeking clarity, one needs to create a tracker and use it religiously. As such, there needs to be a review of this habit of seeking clarity on a periodic basis.

Lists: One needs to create a list of activities that need to be done as far as seeking clarity is concerned. This should be easy because it comes from the earlier habits of discovery and capture. Your list is made up of activities that buttress your clarity.

Table: This is a timetable of sorts. It shows you what activity will be carried out when. Seeking clarity is not just about being theoretical. It is also about doing something.

Charts: If you track your actions long enough, it is easy to generate a chart of progress. Nothing inspires you more personally than seeing a progression of growth in your charts. Nothing holds you accountable more than realizing that you must either maintain or enhance your current performance levels.

Innovation: anything good is worth improving upon. We innovate when we are in motion, at least with something that is already in existence.

Installing the habit: The most powerful consistency with habits is daily practice. A habit is practiced consistently. There are different actions that can be taken to make it consistent and periodic. Of course, not all actions can be taken daily. However, as indicated in the following table, there are different actions that we need to take so that seeking clarity as a habit is installed in our lives.

	Once	**Daily**	**Weekly**	**Monthly**	**Yearly**
Discovery	✓				
Review		✓	✓	✓	✓
Retreat					✓
Prayer		✓			
Journaling		✓			
Meditation		✓			

Figure 2: Review table of clarity of life

Finding clarity is foundational, it is the basic building block for leading a successful and impactful life. There is no point of taking action without clarity. In fact, scripture admonishes us that, 'Even zeal is not good without knowledge, and he who hurries his footsteps misses the mark.'

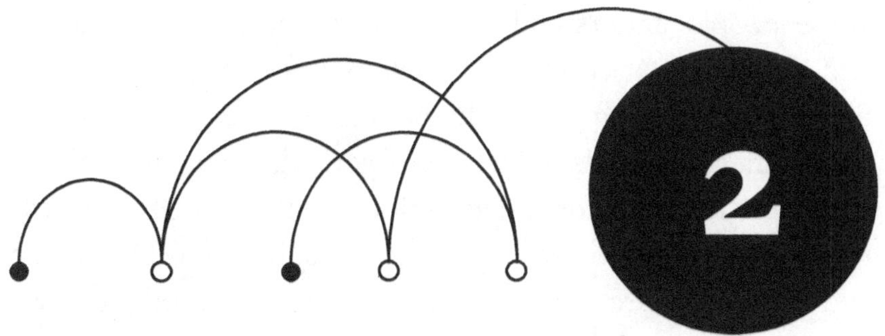

Habit 2: Self-Belief

In the evil, shameful and infamous book Miseducation of the Negro, Carter Godwin Woodson penned down a piece relating to the habit of Self-Belief.

If you can control a man's thinking, you do not have to worry about his action. When you determine what a man shall think, you do not have to concern yourself about what he will do. If you make a man, feel that he is inferior, you do not have to compel him to accept an inferior status, for he will seek it himself.

If you make a man, think that he is justly an outcast, you do not have to order him to the back door. He will go without being told; and if there is no back door, his very nature will demand one.

Some people understand the immense power of self-belief, and if you do not educate yourself, will use it against you by deliberately causing you to doubt your abilities. They will use "innocent" questions such as are you sure you can achieve that goal? Are you not too ambitious? Do you really have the resources and networks to get those results? Self-doubt, fear, and ignorance are cancerous and have even brought down empires.

One that comes to mind was the newly formed kingdom, Israel, many years ago. Their first king, Saul, had an incredible level of self-doubt due to a series of events. At some point, his entire army cowered and hid from their enemies at the battlefield. For forty days, they were taunted and ridiculed by a champion of the enemy force Goliath. How ironic that forty days of hearing taunts from your enemies can make you believe those taunts. This is how some people are subdued. What they hear becomes an inner wiring that fires automatic beliefs which work against them.

Thankfully, there was a champion on Saul's side, but he wasn't in the army. He was a young boy with a habit of conquering. We know this because he told the king that he could kill the giant Goliath *the same way he had killed a lion and a bear*. David's self-belief was sky-high because he already had some victories under his belt. At the end of the day, it was exactly as David confidently predicted — he killed Goliath.

Several years ago, I decided to resign from my job and form a private company. Upon receiving my resignation letter, my supervisor told me that I did not have a natural disposition to run a private business and that I was more suited for the managerial position I held.

In fact, she even expressed this view to other employees at the company. She also engaged me in an hour-long lecture about competition for a limited number of customers and the headaches of running a private company. Her trash counseling temporarily created self-doubt in me. I had spent two solid months drawing up a detailed business plan and could not allow this distraction to derail my vision. Moreover, I was just proud enough not to retract my resignation.

I went on to build successful companies and literally earn over a thousand times more than my salary at the time. If I had accepted my supervisor's "advice," I would still be earning an average salary and leading an average life devoid of adventure and purpose. I would possibly have never written this and other books.

Millions of people have been discouraged from acting on a brilliant idea that could have changed the world- they caved in because they did not believe in themselves. Self-confidence, faith, and self-belief are *being* habits. They form your personality, value system, and seat of passion. They are internal forces.

The African saying admonishes us that, 'If the enemy within has been conquered, the enemy without can do us no harm.'

Our inner state of confidence is intact when we are born and yet to interact with failure, hate, comparisons, competition, pressure to fit in, longing for acceptance, fear of failure, rejection, and other external factors affect our self-belief.

A cocktail of fears, doubts, prejudices, and limitations are gradually injected in our lives by our parents, teachers, relatives, and the media. With all these external factors, we get corrupted, and our sense of faith, belief, and self-esteem is gradually eroded.

Self-belief is not static. It keeps evolving, either positively or negatively, depending on what we do or don't do. That's why it is a habit and not a trait or a talent. We have to pick it up every day and polish it.

The ultimate test of self-belief is your faith. Faith in yourself, your reason for existence, and the hope for a brighter future. You will be amazed by how many people don't believe that they are born equipped to be happy, successful, prosperous, and how low people think of themselves, how much disbelief they have about their prospects in life.

People are for the most part sleepwalking through life because their sense of faith in themselves and the hope for the future is minimal to none.

People who have a healthy sense of self-belief and faith are the ones who dare mighty things. They are able to pick themselves up whenever they fail and give a second trial until they succeed.

Interestingly, those people who have Habit 1 (Seeking Clarity) already installed in their lives, tend to have a healthy sense of self-belief and faith.

One of the biggest aspects of this habit is the penchant to be excited about the invisible, intangible things of promise that are yet to materialize. It is the ability to lurch onto ideas that one is passionate about and gestate them.

The good news is that we can always learn to be more self-confident. There are things that we can do to increase our levels of self-belief.

Self-Awareness: Not only must we know that we are here on earth for a mission and that we are needed, but we must also believe that if we have a low sense of self-awareness, then it follows that we shall have a low level of faith and belief. Therefore, knowledge and belief are essential here.

Just like the habit of seeking clarity, self-awareness is not something that is done once, and you forget about it. We must learn to choose it over self-doubt on a daily basis. One of the tools that can be used to daily power up this habit is "affirmations."

Create a positive, powerful affirmation devoid of negatives. "I am not a mistake" is not a good affirmation because your mind focusses on the word "Mistake." "I am unique, needed and wanted" are more powerful than "I am not a mistake."

Dare the Impossible: Self-belief and faith are developed in two ways that go in tandem. The first is the spiritual part of accepting possibilities. The second is the physical part of doing the "impossible."

We need to be smart here. Impossibilities are not the things that are outside of your capacity. For the most part, they are those things within your realm of passion and purpose, but they will need you to stretch yourself beyond your average daily appearance in life.

If you are a classroom teacher, an impossibility could be to own a chain of high-end schools, for instance. If you already own a school, an impossibility could be to build more regionally and even own several universities across the world. These in fact are not impossible tasks.

The more we dare, even if we fail, the more we are growing in confidence. The most potent intelligence or feedback you get in life is not what you have read in a book. It is the feedback that you get first-hand through attempting something whether you succeed or fail. The more of such feedback you get, the better person you are becoming. You are becoming self-confident, courageous, and full of belief.

Detachment from Failure: Shame, embarrassment, rejection, loss of resources, and time, are just but part of the many things that we risk getting when we go on a "dare date." Self-belief is not a guarantee that there will be no setbacks. It is, in fact, an acknowledgment that despite these things, you are determined to stand up whenever you fail.

Period	What to Dare
This Month	
This Quarter	
This Year	
5 Years	
10 Years	
20 Years	

Figure 3: Table specifying what and when to dare

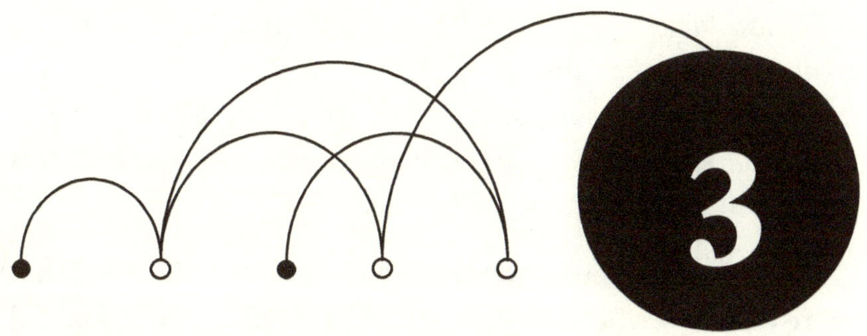

Habit 3: Determination and Persistence

It was not funding, but determination that made the Wright brothers discover flight. They had barely any financing resources, but it is true that the greatest resource they had was intangible, spiritual, and resided in their hearts. Today the aviation industry is worth over USD 110 billion and employs millions of people all over the world.

In his "Moon Speech," the 35th President of the United States envisaged the impossibilities that they would encounter and yet looked right past them by the power of determination when he uttered these words:

We choose to go to the moon. We choose to go to the moon in this decade and do other things, not because they are easy, because it is hard...because that challenge is one, we are willing to accept, one we are unwilling to postpone, and one we intend to win and do others too.

To put this speech in context, you will need to understand that there was no verified technology to take a man to the moon and land him back safely. However, JFK set a timeframe by saying, 'This decade.' This was sheer determination. It is reported severally that such a vision that was cast with so much passion invigorated even the butlers at the National Aeronautics and Space Administration, NASA.

When asked what they were doing, their response wasn't something like, "I am sweeping" or anything mindless to that effect. They emphatically would say, 'I am sending a man on the moon.' Perhaps the question that we need to answer is 'why do we need determination as a habit?'

Why determination?

Because it is the path to greatness: If you are interested in being a great person in any niche of life, you will do that only through the path of determination. This is not necessarily the strategy because we have seen people who are well-intentioned and determined failing. However, without determination, there will be no strategy, no will, and no spirit to pursue anything. Therefore, determination is preceded by direction, desire, calling, goal, purpose, or objective.

I was determined to become a lawyer way before high school, but there were a few challenges I had to overcome before my dream could come true.

My school was subpar, and no student in the previous five years had qualified to study law. Secondly, my parents could not afford to pay the university tuition for a law course. I did not have adequate career guidance to direct me on which paths and options I had to study law. The school had inadequate study material for one to excel and many of the teachers in the school were demotivated and ill-equipped to assist their students achieve the best possible grades.

I decided to study one of the subjects on my own and convinced the headmistress to allow me to register for that particular subject. That meant that I had to come up with a unique study timetable and work much harder than other students. Indeed, I was the only student in the entire school who sat for that subject. I passed my exams with straight As and was one of the best students in the country, qualified to study law on a government scholarship. It's now over 23 years and no student has yet equaled or broken my academic record in that school.

My narrative is an attestation that determination has a target, a far-reaching future objective that is massive enough to require resources and efforts, and capacities that might not be present at the moment. Merriam-Webster Dictionary does great justice to the definition of the word "determination."

: the act of deciding definitely and firmly.

: firm or fixed intention to achieve a desired end.

Therefore, determination doesn't exist in a vacuum. It is pegged on something. This "something" is what Viktor E Frankl called "a cause greater than oneself." We have covered this in Habit 1. Once we have this clarity of what matters to us, we know that for it to be fulfilled, the habit of determination will be the conveyor belt that we shall use to propel us to where we want to go.

I strongly feel that determination is a "being" habit, one that needs to be inculcated in us so much so that it is automatic. It shouldn't be a habit espoused by a select few because of their genes or personality. It should be a human habit because all humans are goal-seeking.

Because there is opposition: Monty Roberts' story has been told over and over again, and I will repeat it here. He was raised by a father who used to move from one horse stable to another as his work was training horses. As such, he missed out on school, or at least his schooling was interrupted several times. One day, a teacher asked him to write about his desires, and what he wanted to do when he grew up.

Monty filled up seven pages detailing a dream that he wanted to own a ranch. He even drew stables as he envisioned them, talked about the location of the buildings and everything he needed on his ranch.

The teacher was not amused. He gave Monty an F. When He protested, the teacher told him that the dreams were so unrealistic for a boy like him who had no money or resources to actualize them. The teacher told him that there was no possibility to reach his goals. He asked him to redo the work and write a different dream.

Monty conferred with his father who asked him to make his own decision on what he wanted to do. The following day, he returned the same paper to the teacher unchanged. 'You can keep your F, and I will keep my dream,' he told the teacher. Today, Monty Roberts owns a 4,000-square-foot house in the middle of a 200-acre ranch. His paper is framed and hangs near his fireplace.

As sure as the sun rises every day, you will face opposition to your dreams and desires. In fact, you will face opposition from yourself, loved ones, and from strangers. The antidote is determination.

Because of the need to grow in capacity: The natural mode for humans in life is not intentional growth. It is drifting. We don't get in life things because we are good, deserving, or God-fearing. We get things because we have deliberately chosen to grow. Determination helps us to grow in our capacity and in stature so that we can qualify for better things in life.

Because it is a principle of life: When all is said and done, determination is woven into the principles of life for all the living things. For human beings, nobody is alive, survives, thrives, and makes a difference without being determined. It is a life principle for success.

Calvin Coolidge, the 30th President of the United States, had this to say about determination:

Nothing in this world can take the place of persistence. Talent will not; nothing is more common than unsuccessful men with talent. Genius will not; unrewarded genius is almost a proverb. Education will not; the world is full of educated derelicts. Persistence and determination alone are omnipotent. The slogan "Press On!" has always and will solve the problems of the human race.

This quote gives a conviction that determination ranks so high up there on the habits that humans need to have, at least according to a man who led one of the most powerful countries.

It's an all-weather habit: Kevin Hall, in his book Aspire, tells a powerful story of Chad Hymas. Chad became a quadriplegic in a split second while working in the farm. The bale of hay he was lifting with his tractor ended up falling on his neck, pinning him to the steering wheel. His life was saved, but he was forever sentenced to a wheelchair. This is a man whose life was "normal" in one minute and the next minute, the word "vegetative" comes to mind.

What lifts us up above from such tragedies? The answer would be personal determination.

Chad Hymas was paralyzed from neck down. His dreams and plans for his life and family were forever shattered. He had to change the trajectory of his life, and looking for options, he zeroed in on public speaking. His coach would be Kevin Hall, the author of that wonderful book, Aspire.

For him to make it as one of the greatest speakers ever, Chad Hymas needed to do something tangible, some kind of physical evidence that would give him credibility that he had what it takes to conquer adversity; the more dramatic, demanding, and memorable, the better. The dream for his career was "to deliver a message that would encourage and inspire others to follow their dreams.

To pull this off, they decided that Chad would be the first quadriplegic to ride a wheelchair from Salt Lake City to Las Vegas in the heat of summer, some 513 miles away. This is close to one thousand kilometers, some 825.593 kilometers. He would do this alone. He did, but not without drama. The weather was against him. He had to do it with loneliness.

There was a heavy leaning towards giving up. What held the man to his own goal was the spirit of determination. When the crowds that waved him off at the starting line and the police escort left him and he was just alone, the companion that he leaned on was determination.

An organization, upon hearing his exploits, booked him to deliver a speech three days later! Since then, he became a sought-after speaker.

For all the habits that have been covered in this book, determination is one that makes each of them a reality.

Two daily questions that you need to ask yourself are: What am I aspiring for? What am I overcoming?

Day	**What Am I aspiring for?**	**What am I overcoming?**
Monday		
Tuesday		
Wednesday		
Thursday		
Friday		
Saturday		
Sunday		

Figure 4: Table specifying aspirations

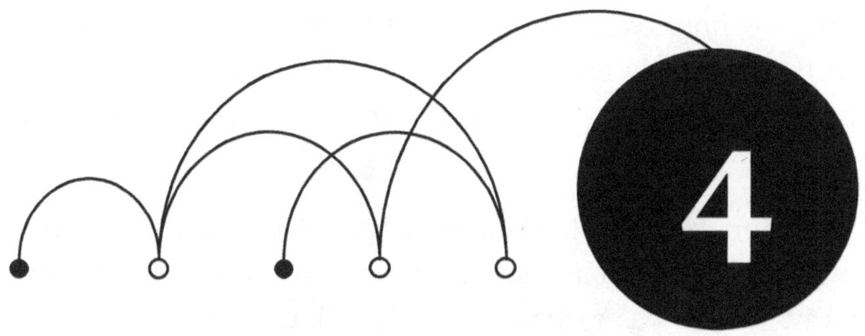

Habit 4: Integrity

In his book, *The Man Who Listens to Horses*, Monty tells us a beautiful story about integrity. Early on as he desired to be a horse trainer, he only had four horses to train. The income from those was not enough. He needed more and he needed to get established.

One day, he was presented with an opportunity to work with a horse trainer called Don Dodge. Don was extending a ten-week apprenticeship to Monty. He asked Monty to go with two of his horses. After the apprenticeship, Don told Monty to tell the owner of one of the horses that he was wasting time and money on it.

That the horse wouldn't amount to anything. That was bitter truth to swallow for Monty because it meant that there was one horse less to train and therefore, less money to earn. What would he do?

Monty braced himself when he delivered the news to the horse owner who was not amused. He called him names and sent him away. Monty was satisfied to have followed the instructions that he was given. A few days later, his phone rang. A friend to the horse owner informed him that he had heard of what had happened. He further said that he had come to believe that Monty was one of the fewest faithful and truthful people in town. He would have loved to send him his horse for training. That's how Monty's fortunes began to grow so much so that he ended up being the trainer of Queen Elizabeth's horses.

Now, there is no knowing what would have happened were he not to tell the truth about the horse, the bitter truth for that matter. Monty showed integrity.

At the start of our legal practice, we were approached by a gentleman who wanted to appeal a case he had lost. Upon examination of the documentation that he presented; we concluded that the trial judge had made the right decision. We communicated our analysis to him, and he was very unhappy because he expected us to support his views that he had been unfairly treated by the trial judge. Fast forward, he found lawyers who were willing to file an appeal on his behalf and subsequently lost the case at the court of appeal.

However, he was gracious enough to come back to us and thank us for telling him the truth. In appreciation, he gave us an art piece which we hung in our board room as a reminder to all who work with us to provide accurate and truthful analysis to all who seek our advice.

There is a cost to integrity. However, at the same time, there is a reward for it. The problem is that the cost is immediate, but the prize is uncertain.

However, the instant benefit of integrity when you have been tested and passed is that you receive peace of mind that cannot be quantified in human terms.

The consequences of integrity can be witnessed in the story of US President Richard Nixon, who willfully oversaw the breaking of the Democratic National Committee Headquarters at the Washington DC Watergate Office Building. In the subsequent months, he directly participated in the cover-up and used White House resources to do so. He ended up resigning as President of the United States of America over one thing — lack of integrity.

Think of traits associated with lack of integrity and tell me if you would love to have a relationship of any kind with a person that has any of these:

Deceitfulness,

Fraudulence,

Lying,

Untruthfulness,

Corruption,

Treachery,

Duplicity,

Cheating

Trickery.

The scripture tells us that, 'A good name is to be chosen rather than great riches, loving favor, rather than silver and gold.'[3] To "choose a good name" is simply to have integrity habits in our being. When we go after silver and gold at the expense of our name or reputation, we know for sure that we are doing wrong. Our hearts will tell us as much. Integrity outlasts our lives yet silver and gold fade away.

Practicing integrity

For integrity to be a "being" habit in us, we need to have some clarity about it. The following are some of the things that we can do to increase the level of integrity in our lives.

Get a moral code/values: The beginning of integrity is to get a moral code that defines what you stand for. This could be in a religious book or a philosophy that does not only benefit you, but other people and the universe.

---

3 Proverbs 22:1

Announce them: Once you have clarified your moral code, it is imperative that you tell the world about it. This is so that you can be held accountable. Announcing your moral code empowers you to walk the talk. When you see someone publicly identifying themselves as Buddhist, Moslem, Humanist, or Christian, what they have done is to announce part of their moral code.

It means that you ought to hold them in the highest regard of that moral code. We announce our values on our website so that the public can know what we stand for and can hold us accountable.

Learn to say no: "No" is a very powerful word. Even though it is negative, it has helped us get protection from harm and enabled us to maintain boundaries. Living with integrity will mean that you will have to say "No" several times for the very reason that your integrity might not be appreciated by everyone.

Choose your company: Find men and women of like passions, people who have a similar moral code, and include them in your life.

There is a special group of people, popularly referred to as "the inner circle" that you and I need in our lives. When the preacher Billy Graham set out early in his ministry, he got a band of brothers with whom he shared a moral code. This code was concerning money, women, and ministry. They held each other accountable to that code.

Nearly a century later, there is not a single accusation against the late Billy Graham on any matters regarding this moral code being flouted.

Pay the price: In the year 2005, Andy Roddick was playing against Fernando Verdasco in the round of 16 at the Italia Masters in Rome, Italy. Being on the third match point, Roddick wasn't able to return a hard second serve from Fernando. The umpire deemed it to be out and awarded the point to Roddick.

The crowds congratulated him and even Fernando ran to the net to shake his hand. Andy Roddick though, knew what Fernando, the umpire, and the crowds did not. The ball was in. He walked to the umpire and reported as much, willing to show where the ball had hit and left a mark. The umpire reversed the call and awarded Fernando the point. The Spaniard went ahead and won the match, dumping Andy Roddick out of the tournament. Andy paid the price for his integrity, and in so doing, lost tens of thousands of dollars and perhaps lost more if he would have gone on to win the tournament.

There is no telling when you will be put to the test but when that happens, the litmus test of your integrity is when you are willing to lose tangibles for the sake of the unseen — your integrity.

Turn-Around: We started this chapter by talking about Richard Nixon. Perchance you fail your own test of integrity, one more thing that you can do is acknowledge your wrong. Reaffirm your commitment to your moral code, apologize and set on the journey back to it. That's where the freedom is. What Richard Nixon did was the complete opposite. He continued denying his lack of integrity until he could not do so anymore. He was forced to resign and yet he went out of office completely humiliated.

The point is that he had an opportunity very early on to own up and make a change. He didn't. Were it not for his successor, Henry Ford to pardon him, Richard Nixon would have moved from the White House to prison. Think about that. Today, all manner of examples of lack of integrity in leadership are always about Richard Nixon.

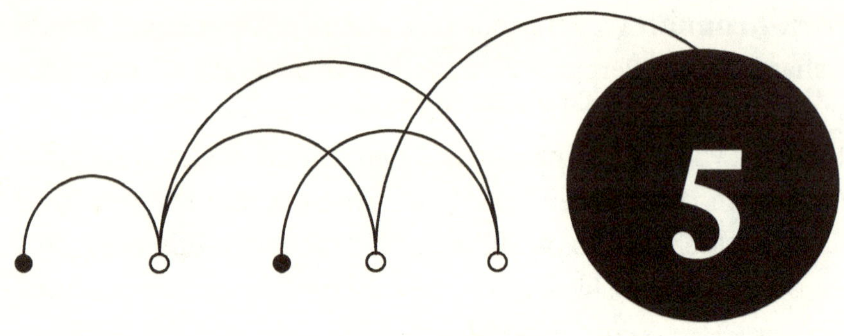

Habit 5: Self - Discipline

American Clergyman Harry Emerson Fosdick who lived between 1878 and 1969 said: *No horse gets anywhere until he is harnessed. No stream or gas drives anything until it is confined. No Niagara is ever turned into light and power until it is tunneled. No life ever grows great until it is focused, dedicated, and disciplined.*

Basically, nothing transformative, progressive, creative, or revolutionary happens unless there is self-discipline.

What kind of person would you be if there were no consequences for your action? What would you gravitate towards? I can speculate what kind of person you would be. In fact, you have been that person at one point in your life.

We all have been there, we have all been babies. There is no need whatsoever for a baby to be self-disciplined. In fact, the major differentiation between a baby and an adult is self-discipline.

The Cambridge Dictionary gives a wonderful explanation for the word "self-discipline": *the ability to make yourself do things you know you should do even when you do not want to.*

In talking about self-discipline, the keyword, we have to realize, is "self." It is an individual thing, seldom a group, corporate, or club thing.

Virtually everything you have today and the person you are becoming is a by-product of self-discipline or lack of it. Every dream you have worth pursuing will be realized through self-discipline. The quality of life we live is directly proportional to the amount of self-discipline that we practice.

We need self-discipline to live within our means, save money and invest it. You cannot wear this habit once in a while and put it off at will. This is another "being" habit. It directly impacts your identity, your core, and your being.

I dare say that self-discipline or lack of it thereof is the reason why we have leadership. I do not think man was designed to rule over another man or a man was designed to be subservient to another.

If all of us exercised our self-discipline to the uttermost, there would be no need for police, prisons, judges, and lawyers like myself. Most of the things we litigate about always have at their core the element of someone missing the mark of self-discipline.

On the other hand, it is obvious to see that whatever that is thriving, whatever is transforming, whatever that is impacting this world, if there is any personal growth and grandeur, if there is individual or collective achievement, self-discipline has always been responsible for it

Self-discipline also helps us to avoid harmful situations like alcoholism, drug abuse and other addictions.

Why is self-discipline important?

Brings self-control and stability: There is no self-control in your life if you lack discipline and you will in turn not be productive.

A life of stability is the side effect of the habit of self-discipline. If you want to see the depth of this truth, ask someone who is addicted to something. At the deepest part of their heart, they long for stability. Self-discipline has the power to deliver it.

Creates stability and growth: When you take the reins of your life through self-discipline, there is a level of stability that you welcome into your life. It is important for your progress and growth.

Protects us from distractions: We are living in the most distracted world ever since the beginning of time. We are able to access social media, TV and live events at any one time on our phones and gadgets. This affects our creativity and productivity. Self-discipline is the greatest habit that we have to avoid such distractions.

How to cultivate self-discipline?

Self-discipline doesn't happen by itself. The following are the pointers to use as you build your self-discipline.

Focus: Refer to Habit 1 on clarity. It gives you the object or the substance or the reason for inculcating self-discipline in your life. As usual, self-discipline has to be towards something that you are doing. If you don't have focus, direction, or desire, the need for having self-discipline is minimized.

Count the cost: Sit down and create a mental image on paper of what it takes to keep your self-discipline. What things will you have to forego? What friendships will you have to end? To be self-disciplined is to know with some level of clarity what you must do and prepare mentally to do it.

Postpone and Schedule Pleasure: Learn to schedule moments of pleasure, relaxation, and rest. These could be distractions if not scheduled. Discipline is about foregoing the pleasures of now so that you can apply yourself to something worthwhile even if it is not pleasurable at the moment. The people who have learnt to schedule pleasure will always do well with their self-discipline.

— PART 2 —

Mind Habits

Mind habits refer to the intentional, intense, conscious, and "present" activities that we engage in that help us not only to survive the day, but to stretch and deploy most of the potential that we have within us. Mind habits are not about intelligence. They are about the will. As such, all human beings have the ability to practice mind habits.

If you were to gather all the successful souls in any niche all over the world, you will realize that none of them got where they are without the use of mind habits. Success is totally predicated on mind habits. That's why Teddy Roosevelt said that *"nothing is more common than unsuccessful men with talent."* If you ever wanted to be successful, whether you are a genius or not, talented, or not, there is no way you are getting there without the application of mind habits.

In his book, *Brain Rules*, John Medina teaches us 12 principles of surviving and thriving at work, home, and school. It is instructive to learn that whatever we do to feed the brain and exercise it, gives power to our mind. In so doing, it leads us to being better and more productive in life. I will restrict myself to just four mind habits that I believe are foundational to our success, growth, and prosperity.

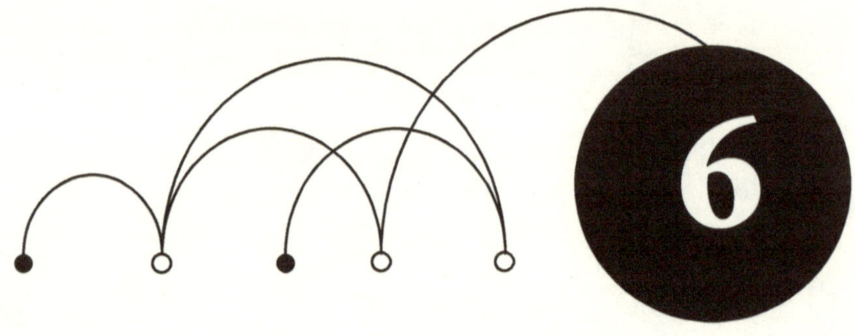

Habit 6: Preparation

The year was 2004. People of Illinois had already been introduced to and knew the pedigree of their Senate candidate. The rest of the world still had not been made aware of the exploits of a certain young man, a lawyer, who was an excellent community organizer. At that time, the United States of America was undergoing the normal electioneering process.

As the Democratic National Convention was taking place, the name of this "nobody" went forth as the one who would make the keynote address. The world was not ready for that day. But the "nobody" had been preparing for it for ages. Barack Obama took to the podium and in sixteen or so minutes, he was introduced to the world.

So potent was his speech that four years later, John McCain, the Republican nominee for President of the United States was still accusing Obama of bringing up the 2004 speech to the campaign. Obama would make history in 2008 to become the first president of color in the United States of America.

There is no question about Obama's gift and talent. He has delivered countless speeches that have mesmerized us all. However, if you were to boil down his "success" to one thing, you will see that the most unlikely of people to become president made it through sheer preparation over the years. His preparation might not have been seen when he was at it, but we are definitely seeing him bask in the glory of those preparations.

Planning and preparedness ought to be a habit that we teach ourselves and espouse in our lives. Highly successful people are consummate planners, and sticklers of preparedness. Preparedness is intentionally setting aside some time to first of all get the insight, the reason behind what you want to do, and then organizing the events to get it done.

The Ant Philosophy is a reminder that planning, and preparedness is a cycle of seasons and not an event.

Ants Never Quit

Ants Think Winter All Summer

Ants Think Summer All Winter

Gather All They Possibly Can in Summer [4]

I do perceive that regardless of someone's background, intellect, or even personality or anything that you could mention that might be an impediment to success, if they developed the habit of planning and preparedness, not just to avert disaster but to maximize their potential, they are destined to succeed.

Getting this habit in your life is as simple as 1,2,3, but it's not necessarily that easy. Use the process below:

Plan: Make it a habit to plan. For this to be feasible, it is important to create weekly plans that can be reviewed daily. Your plans should cover all the important areas of your life including business, finances, relationships, health, relaxation, and the mind. In one sitting, decide what your week is going to look like. This should be in tandem with your clarity and purpose in life.

Track: Your planning has created action points and intermediate destinations. It has also created timelines, expected output, and resources needed. Your tracker is to see and create a percentage performance score line.

Review: This helps you to see if you over-estimated, over-stretched, or better yet, if you under-estimated yourself. To review is to use last week's input to form a better strategy. Suffice it to say, the preparedness habit has to be done on paper and online.

---

4 The Ant Philosophy, Jim Rohn articles

We have very many tools today that we can use. The most powerful app on your smartphone is the calendar app. Use it to create your own appointments, making sure that each hour of the day is planned for.

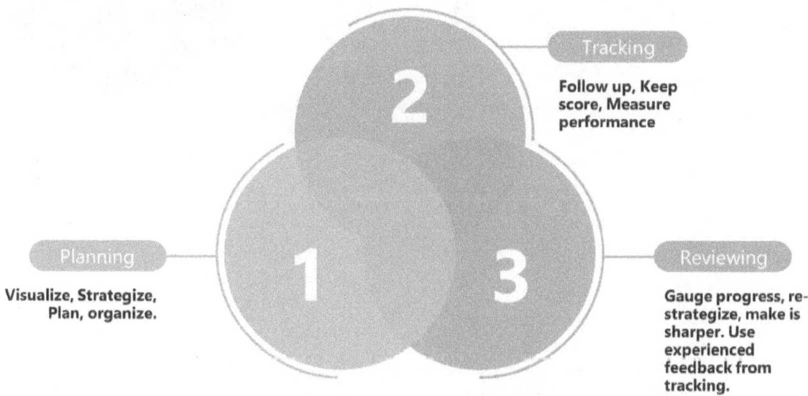

Figure 5: The Preparedness Habit

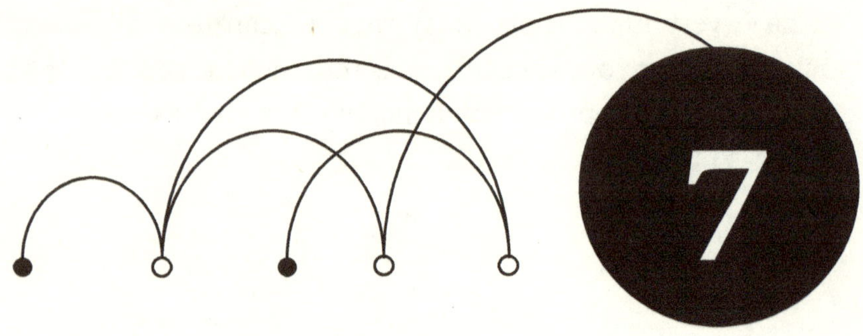

Habit 7: Focus

The snow covered the ground, and three young boys were playing in it. A man said to them, 'Would you like to try to race, with the promise of a prize for the winner?'

The boys agreed, and the man told them that his race was to be different. 'I will go to the other side of the field,' he said, 'and when I give you the signal, you will start to run. The one whose footsteps are the straightest in the snow will be the winner.'

As the race commenced, the first boy began looking at his feet to see if his steps were straight. The second lad kept looking at his companions to see what they were doing, but the third boy just ran on with his eyes fixed on the man on the other side of the field.

The third boy was the winner, for his footsteps were straight in the snow. He had kept his eyes on the goal ahead of him[5].

It has been said that F.O.C.U.S is an acrostic for "Follow. One. Course. Until. Successful." The first boy broke his focus by looking at his feet. The second broke his focus by looking at his companions. The third won by concentrating on the target. The story directly mirrors our lives when we do not focus on achieving particular goals.

Focus is not only a mind habit, but it is also a very powerful productivity hack. Central to failure in people's lives, even those who are geniuses is broken focus. In the world today, unless you have a ruthless streak of focus as a habit, you will be lost in the many distractions around you.

One of the most striking examples of focus in the bible is in Joshua 23:6-7 when Joshua while giving his fare well address advises the Israelites thus "be very firm, then, to keep and do all that is written in the book of the law of Moses, so that you may not turn aside from it to the right hand or to the left..."

Focus is a mental-toughness trait that delivers success. It is true that all around us, we are surrounded by boundless possibilities. However, if we attempt to go after all these possibilities at once we lose direction and achieve none of the many possibilities.

---

5 Rick Meyers, E-Sword 2000+ Illustrations for Preaching

Our ability to finish what we started is strongly influenced by sustaining focus that we have built. While reflecting on the subject of focus, consider the following.

Lack of direction: As mentioned in the story at the introduction of this chapter, the boy who had direction is the one who won the prize. That's how powerful focus is. Inherently, focus is the result of having direction. You cannot focus if there is no direction and clarity of purpose.

Living a life without direction makes you have a very weak muscle to focus. You will find that you are confused, doing many things, and never really getting to finish them. When you get the direction in life, however, it gives you the power, strong enough to focus because there is a clear path to take and a clear reason for taking that path.

Greed and fear: In the personal development world, people talk about "shiny objects" a lot. These are the things that you see when you get your eyes off the target. Shiny objects are things that are not necessarily negative. They are things that you could use. I tend to think, though, that central to following these shiny objects is the trait of greed and desire to get things done and delivered to you without going through the process. The trait of greed has seen people leaving great paths to follow those which promise overnight success such as Ponzi schemes. Thus, their focus is broken by their internal greed. These will prey on your fear and greed.

Impatience: At times, results take longer to manifest than we had envisioned. It is like the boy who planted a grain of maize and kept digging it up to see if it was growing due to his impatience.

In the process, the maize seed that was germinating was interfered with and died. There are multiple stories all over of people who gave up when they were on the verge of a breakthrough. Had they stayed focused just a little bit longer, they would have attained the objective of their goals.

Perhaps the simplest way to inculcate the focus habit is to look at the end result — finishing something. To foster the habit of focus, become a finisher. Push yourself all the time to finish what you started and to start what's worth finishing.

Every morning, answer this question:

'What Must I finish today?'

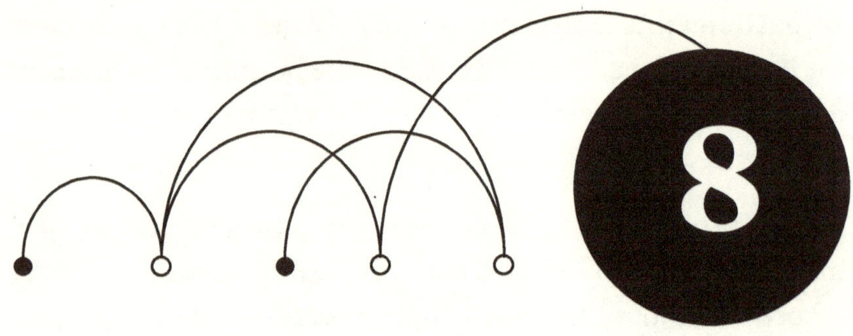

Habit 8: Positive Mental Attitude

The longer I live, the more I realize the impact of attitude on life. Attitude, to me, is more important than facts. It is more important than the past, than education, than money, than circumstances, than failures, than successes, than what other people think, say, or do. It is more important than appearance, giftedness, or skill. It will make or break a company, a church, or a home.

The remarkable thing is, we have a choice every day regarding the attitude we will embrace for that day. We cannot change our past; we cannot change the fact that people will act in a certain way.

We cannot change the inevitable. The only thing we can do is play on the one string that we have, and that is our attitude.

I am convinced that life is 10 percent what happens to me and 90 percent how I react to it. And so, it is with you. We are in charge of our attitudes. — Charles Swindoll.

A positive mental attitude is one of the most critical tools we can use in life. At times, people scoff at this because they have a wrong perception of positive mental attitude, popularly referred to as "PMA."

People wrongly think that PMA is about negating the reality and delving into the land of utopia. In fact, the very reason we need PMA is because of the harsh realities that we face.

The thread in this book with all the habits we are discussing is about success and excelling in life. Again, if you looked at the greatest visionaries this world has ever seen and scrutinized their lives, you will easily find out that they are men and women with a great PMA. On the other hand, millions of people are unemployed, underemployed, and have bad interpersonal relationships because of having a negative mental attitude.

PMA kept Nelson Mandela alive while he was imprisoned by the racist apartheid regime for 27 years. His dream of a liberated South Africa came true during his lifetime. He was able to witness all South Africans participate in a democratic election of their leaders.

The miracle of PMA made him the first president of a liberated South Africa. PMA should be used even when there is no crisis.

That's why I am advocating for it to be a habit. If it can help someone out of a crisis, it surely can help someone to stretch and become better than they are today. One of the biggest mistakes we make with our lives is to wait until a crisis wakes us up.

When it does, we are normally astounded at the things that we would be able to accomplish under pressure. The problem is that a crisis at times comes once in a blue moon. If we were to bank on a crisis for a wake-up call, the rest of our lives would not take advantage of the opportunities that are already available around us. That's why a positive mental attitude is critical to our growth. You will hardly find a person with a negative attitude having a grand vision.

Reading something about Elon Musk, there was a time that he and his friends went to Russia trying to either rent or purchase rockets. This giant of a man in terms of attitude was rebuffed by the Russians. On the way back to the airport, his friends were in a somber mood observing the peasants in Russia. On the plane, Musk sat in a row in front of them typing away on his computer.

At this point, Musk wheeled around and flashed a spreadsheet he'd created. 'Hey, guys,' he said, 'I think we can build this rocket ourselves.' This is no mere suggestion; PMA was in action for this guy not to give up.

How to create a Positive Mental Attitude

If perchance you are implementing the habits we are talking about so far, you will easily find that the habit of Positive Mental Attitude (PMA) borrows a lot from the previous habits. The first thing that you need is to have a great direction that you are taking. That's where the habit of seeking clarity comes in. It is the seed for PMA.

You water your PMA seed with the habits of self-belief, preparedness, and focus. You need to believe that you are capable, useful, and necessary in this world. You have to know that you are unique and created to provide a unique solution to the world. You need PMA to achieve your purpose and mission in the world.

Secondly, you have to believe that as long as you are still alive, today is the factory of your dreams and inspired action, so tomorrow can be better than today.

Thirdly, you have to believe in the philosophy of the silver lining:

'Every adversity, every failure, every heartbreak, carries with it the seed of an equal or greater benefit.' — Napoleon Hill.

Dr. G. Campbell Morgan recounts of a man whose shop had been burned in the great Chicago fire. He arrived at the ruins the next morning carrying a table.

He set it up amid the charred debris and above it placed this optimistic sign, *"Everything lost except wife, children, and hope. Business will be resumed as usual tomorrow morning."*

The more you practice PMA, the more you build resilience, mental toughness, and fortitude not only to overcome a crisis but also to thrive and attain future prospects. These are the five pillars of a PMA.

Thoughts: *"Garbage in garbage out"*, this principle does not only apply to computers but to humans too. What you think about yourself can get clothed in its physical equivalent. If you have negative thoughts, you will have a negative outlook on life even if the environment around you is blessed with opportunities.

Perhaps some of the most powerful thoughts we can have are those of gratitude. It is such a great emotional leveler that it needs to be a daily habit in and of itself. To cultivate thoughts of gratitude is a practical exercise that we need to do daily.

Speech: The most important words are not those that you hear but those that you speak to yourself! We already talked about this in Habit 2 - Self-Belief. The internal dialogue you have with yourself is more powerful than you would ever think. Watch what you say to yourself repeatedly. Anything negative you tell yourself doesn't help foster PMA. In addition to having thoughts of gratitude, also have words of gratitude spoken not just to yourself, but also to other people.

Being grateful creates an environment of positivity for you and for those around you.

Action: Inactivity is as toxic as it gets. If you sat and did nothing, you are likely to have a bad attitude. Activity has a way of releasing the feel-good hormones in our systems and therefore gives a promise, hope, and a feeling that we matter. Whether you are employed or not, make it a habit to be active in life. Find as many avenues to serve humanity as you can. Otherwise, as they say, your mind will become the devil's workshop.

Company: The company you keep has to be of those people that are more positive than yourself. People that are daring. People that have results that you seek, and people that are much. You cannot sacrifice your PMA for belonging. I say this because there are some people that would rather belong to a company that looks down on them, speaks ill of them, prophesies doom about them, and so on. If you want PMA, you need to be active in getting all the negative people out of your life.

Rest: The person that is not well rested, the one that is tired tends to have a short temper. At times, you might push yourself trying to make things happen, but you are seeing no results. This can easily affect your mental attitude especially if you do not take time to go and rest.

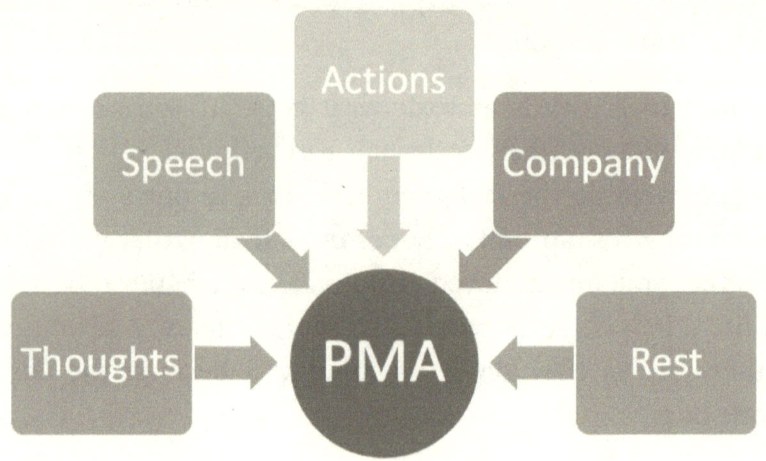

Figure 6: Pillars of Positive Mental Attitude

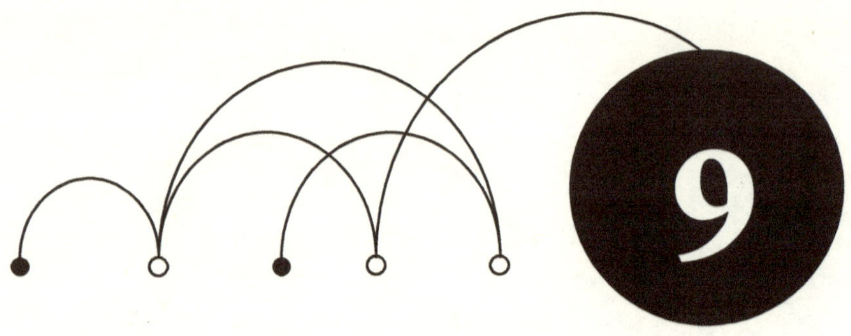

Habit 9: Continuous Self-Education

The Law of Entropy will tell you that if you left your car unattended, unused, and not serviced, it would slowly disintegrate. The same thing happens to our brains when we are no longer stretching them in different ways. One of the ways of stretching our brains is through reading, self-development, and continuous self-education. You cannot leave your brain and mind unattended and expect to be sharp, relevant, and on the cutting edge of success in this fast-paced world.

About ten years after graduating from university, I felt that both my professional and social life had stalled. My finances were in disarray and although I was making a lot of money, I was enslaved by debt.

I had all it took to be successful and wealthy, yet I was leading an average life. I didn't find a clear direction toward a meaningful and successful life until I began to engage in continuous self-education.

The traditional approach to education has created a generation of people who don't value self-education. They stop learning once they leave university. They are misguided that all the knowledge they needed to face this life was obtained in paper qualification. Others only concentrate in reading material in their narrow fields of training. They are not aware that knowledge expires and thus, miss out on valuable skills like self-management, financial literacy, healthy living, and more knew researched information.

Education has been seen to be that which is arduous, restricted, examinable, and rewarded by an event such as a graduation and benefits such as a job. In other words, if you remove the tail end of the process of education, many people will not see the value of going to school.

That's why there are bizarre ceremonies when people are *"through with school"* if you would believe that! There are some people who burn their notes as they watch the bonfire with so much delight and sell of their textbooks at a giveaway price. They are telling their brains that education is over and now they are "free." I might not need to authorize research to know that the percentage of people who picked up a book after graduation is so minimal and heartbreaking.

In the place of a book, people point at their university degree or diploma hanging on a wall. Would you believe it? There are people today seeking to be relevant in life with a university degree that they attained over thirty years ago!

Our cultures glorified education and rightfully so, because when it was instituted, we needed people who could work in offices and industries. That was the sole purpose of education – to produce civil and obedient servants rather than free creative and innovative thinkers.

It still holds true today that if you want to be employed, you will need to have "some papers." What has happened though is that we have had the purpose of education and the meaning of education totally lost. Increasingly, it's becoming a disillusion to acquire the standard education and still be unemployed.

The constant is that the more you engage with continuous self-direction the more relevant knowledge you are to have and likely you are to succeed in any niche in life. You are more likely to start a business as a result of your self-education than to seek out jobs elsewhere that may not exist. There are more qualified individuals than job openings on the market.

There is no end in learning. Jim Ron is famed to have said:

'Formal education will earn you a living; self-education will make you a fortune.'

This habit cannot be overemphasized. It's one of the most important daily habits that we need to inculcate in our lives. Once you know your destination in the future, it is continuous self-education that will deliver you to that destination. What it is about is simply increase in capacity. With continuous self-education, one of the standout principles about it is that it is daily. The second principle is that it is not massive. It is one drop at a time,

Getting it done

- Select a specific area of education. This should be in line with your purpose, career, passion, or vocation.
- Select a related field of study, one that you are interested in.
- Create a list of all the sources of information that you can glean from.
- Create a plan of acquisition and time allocation for all these resources.
- Create a monthly learning timetable.
- Get started.
- Track it.

— PART 3 —

Action Habits

It is important to take informed actions if we are to succeed. An arbitrary action cannot achieve much. You can have your day filled with actions but in the end, they do not contribute to your effectiveness. To be effective is to take impactful action. Just the fact that you are busy doesn't mean that you are being productive. Action habits are all about productivity. They are about maximizing your time, talent, skill, and effort to be the most productive version of yourself.

Bruce Lee famously said, '*I don't fear the person who has practiced ten thousand kicks once, but the person who has practiced one kick ten thousand times.*'

In his book, The Four-Hour Workweek, Tim Ferris weighs in on the subject of efficiency and effectiveness so well:

Here are two truisms to keep in mind:

Doing something unimportant well does not make it important.

Requiring a lot of time does not make a task important.

Action habits will help you full fill your purpose by bringing your ideas to life.

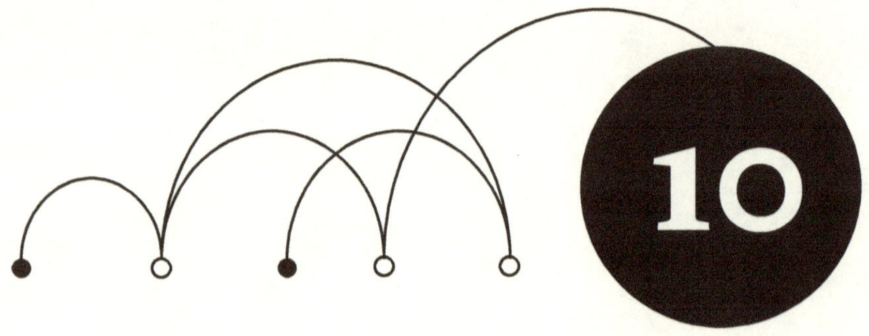

Habit 10: Waking Up Early

One of the most powerful speeches ever delivered and widely quoted was by Theodore Roosevelt back in 1910, commonly referred to as "Man in the Arena" reminds us of the powerful nuggets that he poured out that day:

It is not the critic who counts, not the man who points out how the strong man stumbles, or where the doer of deeds could have done them better. The credit belongs to the man who is actually in the arena, whose face is marred by dust and sweat and blood; who strives valiantly; who errs, who comes short again and again, because there is no effort without error and shortcoming; but who does actually strive to do the deeds; who knows great enthusiasms, the great devotions; who spends himself in a worthy cause; who at the best knows, in the end, the triumph of high achievement, and who at the worst, if he fails, at least fails while daring greatly, so that his place shall never be with those cold and timid souls who neither know victory nor defeat.

Roosevelt is talking about an action-packed human being, who is preferred to the spectator and the critic. It is the man in action that faces the opponent and receives feedback. You cannot be that person if you wake up so late in the day. Listen to this: It matters less whether you are employed or not.

Waking up early sets the pace for the rest of the day and sends signals to your brain and body that you are needed. On the contrary, waking up late also sets a sluggish pace, sending a message to the body that there is no urgency in life.

The attitude and habit of waking up early are important in setting the pace for productivity in your life. Action attracts action and early action attracts early results. It attracts motion and motion is what results in connections and growth.

World beaters have already accomplished six or so tasks on their day before the average people are awake. This is because they make it a habit to wake up early. It is a habit because it has been inculcated and tenaciously installed in their lives.

Early means — the time when most people are not yet awake. Many people agree that early is about 5:00 am.

The idea of *"early"* is to craft for yourself one to two hours to give yourself the best hours of the day to focus on the most critical aspect of your life — that is yourself. You dedicate these two hours to a moment of self-mastery, creativity, reflection, planning, and anchoring yourself for the rest of the day.

It is at this highly productive time that you have peace, tranquility, freshness, and the magic of creativity. Imagine giving yourself this blessing every single day for the rest of your life!

Why wake up early?

To set the tone for the day: The Swahilis of East Africa have a saying: "Siku njema huonekana asubuhi." The equivalent of this is, you can tell the way the day is going to go by the happenings of the morning. It may sound passive, as if you have no control over it, but the deeper meaning is that how you spend your early morning hours will determine how the rest of the day will go.

There is a heaven-and-earth difference between the person that wakes up early and sets the tone for the rest of the day and the person that sleeps late and lackadaisically wakes up late. In the end, a day turns into a month and then a year, and finally a lifetime of a lazy lifestyle. Potentially wasted by just one habit of waking up late.

To achieve momentum: Momentum is a very powerful force. The earlier you get momentum in your life, the better. Oftentimes, if you wake up late, there is a backlog that is waiting for you to clear. You go through the day sacrificing the most important aspects of your life so that you can catch up and at least survive. However, when you start your day early, you start checking off completed tasks in your to-do list.

This not only sets off the momentum, but also releases the feel-good chemicals of dopamine and endorphins. This enables you to be in control of your day and your life – a happy person and fun to be around. The reward is immense, people want to do business with you, make conversations with you and generally find you a person worth connecting with.

How do we get this habit in our system?

Get started: You can have a habit installed in your life immediately. However, you will never have a habit installed in your life if you don't get started. Get enough rest and purpose to sleep early so that you have at least eight hours of rest.

Get an accountability partner: Find someone that can hold you accountable for what you intend to do. Tell them why you would like to start waking up early. Be sincere to them and tell them that it is your weakness if that's true. This person should be someone who cares for you and is already waking up early. Let this mentor check on you each week to see how you are faring.

Give up unproductive activities: Habit 1 will help you discover your purpose and have clarity on the direction you wish your life to take. You now have greater control over your life and practice the habit of self-discipline.

It is now time for you to give up on unproductive habits like watching TV, gossiping, or bar hopping. This allows you enough time to sleep and wake up early.

Expect hardship: Mentally prepare yourself to suffer in the initial days. It is a sacrifice at first. Prepare yourself to get resistance from your brain and your body. It will be foolhardy to think that you will brush through this at the first asking.

This mental preparedness allows you to release different resources to overcome the expected hardship. To be forewarned is to be forearmed. So do not be naïve. However, rejoice with the fact that soon enough, you will be through the hard and rough path as this practice becomes a habit. The people who expect hardship have the power to handle it better than those who think everything will be smooth sailing.

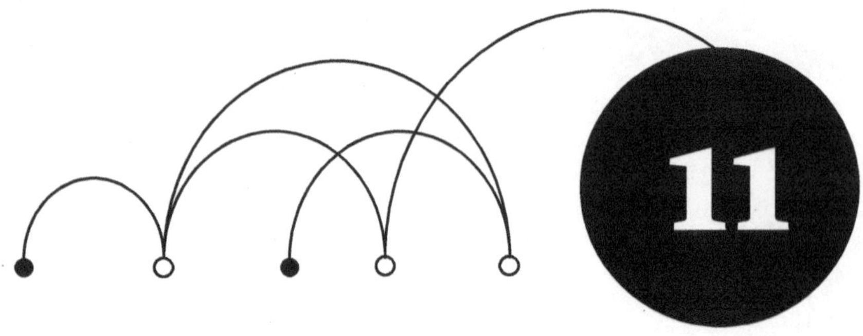

Habit 11: Solve Problems Early

Many years ago, I had a little non-regular pain in one of my teeth which I ignored. After two weeks, the pain became more regular, and I still ignored it. The pain became intense, and I still ignored it. I only went to the dentist when the pain was unbearable... you guessed it right. My tooth was extracted with a warning from the dentist never to wait too long before attending to little problems.

Many diseases are not fatal if detected and acted upon early. If ignored the intensity of the remedy needed becomes costly both in terms of time and financial resources. "A stitch in time saves nine"

Problems are a fact of life. Some are self-inflicted but others are unintentional. Postponing problem-solving doesn't erase it. The nature of a problem is that it is always arduous, uncomfortable, difficult, and demanding. It always speaks of toil, uncertainty, and discomfort. So, we do not want to get our hands dirty. Our brains have always looked out for us, to avoid unhappiness and trouble. Problems signify trouble and the best the brain tells us to do is to run away from it.

Invariably, we have created several excuses that help us not to focus on the problem but the comfort that we can get. That's why some people would rather drink, smoke, or shoot up drugs instead of facing a problem head-on. All the while, these activities are not addressing the problem squarely. Meanwhile, the problem is still there waiting for us. As a matter of fact, it becomes a vicious cycle of addiction because, by the time the "high" we felt wanes off, the problem is staring at us like it never moved. We then go back to look for the high.

We should get into the habit and be willing to confront trouble and problems head-on and at the earliest opportunity. You know the story of the Titanic. On the 15th of April 1912, one thousand five hundred people perished at sea when the Titanic made its maiden voyage from Southampton. The ship was built at a cost of USD 7.5 Million. That's equivalent to over half a billion dollars in value today. It took three years to build this ship, but it only sailed for 4 days. The amazing thing is that you can link this massive tragedy to not solving problems early. Several instances attest to this.

For instance, the titanic was equipped with only twenty-two lifeboats, enough to save only one thousand one hundred people. In actuality, the ship had the capacity to load 64 lifeboats that would have saved three thousand people! The point here is that preparation and anticipation of problems helps us to solve them early before they happen. It beats logic because the designers and engineers of the ship were not prepared enough for the eventuality of the ship getting into trouble at sea.

We are also informed that the Titanic crew received several warnings from other ships about icebergs. They simply ignored these warnings. Chances are that if they had heeded the call, people wouldn't have lost their lives needlessly. A problem was evident, but it was not solved early. The end result was a calamity of untold grief and loss.

Postponing solving a problem almost always guarantees disaster. For one, the problem doesn't go away and as very many variables keep changing, the problem might actually mutate or metastasize into something complex.

We need to grow the habit of solving problems immediately they manifest. Starting to face off with a problem early gives an edge on it.

We get acquainted with what's needed: No doubt, a problem is uncomfortable because we do not know how to solve it. But that can change very easily when we act against it.

Many times, some problems are just compounded by our illusionary interpretation that is coupled with fear. When we do not have enough information about something, it seems as if it is the most difficult thing to resolve. However, all we need to do is to get started, even with the scantest data that we have at our disposal.

You realize that for the most part, problem solving is rather an event than a process. The key is to nip the problem in the bud as early as possible because the longer we wait, the more it grows in complexity. Getting started on it early enables you to be in charge and get as much needed information for the next step towards the solution as possible.

We mentally get moving: Understand that the disposition and state of the mind are critical in problem solving. The more you remain inactive in the face of a problem, the more complex it seems. In fact, the more inactive you are, the more paralyzed you become mentally. Getting started early prepares the mind to start tackling the problem. It is a paradox that the brain would not want you to tackle the problem when it comes, but it is the very same brain that gets so active immediately after you have decided to deal with it.

We build a problem-solving habit that is critical in life: Once we have built a knack of going after a problem head-on, attacking it at the earliest opportunity, we start building a tough muscle in the physical brain and our mental disposition as problem solvers.

We will need this habit over and over again in life. Problems will always be there and the people who have learnt to solve many of them as early as possible are the strongest of the species that exist.

The habit of solving problems early is a master 21st-century skill of success that will not only benefit you but is yearned for by employers.

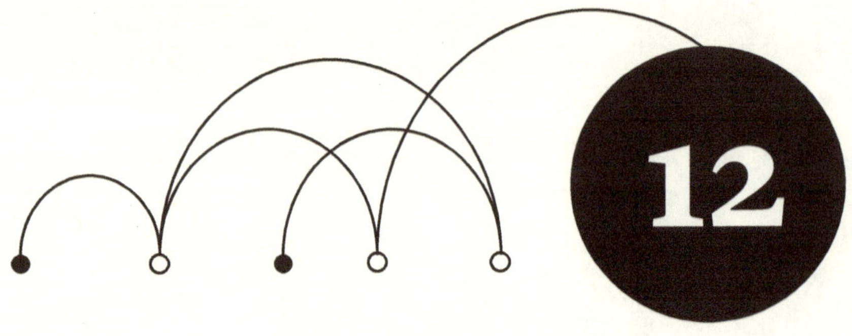

Habit 12: Living Within Your Means

On the 25th of September 2022, 38-year-old marathoner Eliud Kipchoge from Kenya posted an amazing finish at the 2022 BMW Berlin Marathon, in a new world Record Time of 2:01:09. Such a great performance it was that the person who came in next was five minutes late! In November 2022, Eliud Kipchoge was pictured eating a simple meal—rice and beans in a nondescript metal plate.

A debate has been raging among his countrymen about why a man that is as world-famous and wealthy as Eliud would be such frugal with himself.

Aliko Mohammed Dangote is the richest person of African descent. I found out that his great-grandfather, who was a very wealthy merchant in pre-independent Nigeria advised that the successors of his enterprises had to "Live simple, unassuming, frugal lives and steer away from politics."

It is clear that the patriarch of this billionaire family knew the secrets of wealth creation, the spirit of frugality, and living one's life within their means. A life that is not beyond what one can afford.

Every high performer, every person with a cause and with a purpose, has some rules, values, and principles that they apply in order to channel their cause.

We cannot achieve our causes arbitrarily. There will always be a chasm between our wishes and our reality. This occurs especially with financial freedom, which is always going to be bridged by our inspired actions. One of the most potent actions we can take is to live within our means. This is a daily habit we ought to inculcate in our lives.

We have this default mode in our psyches to channel our finances in a one-way traffic—spending. If we do not counter this default 'factory settings' of the human and his relationship with money, we will always have trouble in our finances. The decision to leave within our means is individual and can be arrived at after sincere introspection.

Indeed, there are very many opinions and definitions of living within your means. Some will talk about spending only what you have... others will talk about planning, budgeting, and spending only what someone planned. Merriam-Webster's Dictionary renders it this way:

> Live within one's means: to spend money only on what one can afford

In my opinion, we need to understand the essence of life with clarity and spend money on only the things that matter. Not only must you live within your means but also intentionally ensure that whatever you purchase is among what is necessary and contributes to the achievement of your life's purpose. Being aware of what is necessary will help to avoid shiny objects, fear of missing out, and unwarranted luxuries you cannot afford. To live within your means, you need to practice the lifestyle below.

Get Intentional: If you wanted to know whether you are living within your means, a simple test is to take a look at all your *purchases*, whether habitual or by instinct, and ask yourself this question: What percentage of these expenses were *necessary*?

The major reason we live beyond our means is that we do not have financial discipline. We also do not have a vision or an overriding guiding system for our money; both income and expenditure. Therefore, if you and I want to live our lives within our means, we need to have a plan for income and expenditure.

It is preferable that plan on how to spend money even before you earn it.

There are very many free Apps today that can help you to plan and track your income and expenses as they come. At a glance, you will see how much you have spent in whatever category. You will also see how many streams of income you created and how each fared in that season.

If you wish to live within your means, the first thing that you step is to be intentional about it, make a plan, and religiously track your expenditure.

Be Confident in Yourself: If you were to trace some root causes of people living beyond their means, is that they want to please others. The many items bought by such people are merely to show off in order to purchase acceptance. It could be phones, clothes, cars, houses, name it. All these things are 'temporary appendages' that we think will give us meaning and a sense of fitting in a particular group. We could do well without them.

Greed, Fear, and Impatience: These are other inert factors that contribute to living a life beyond your means. Every day, we are bombarded with opportunities to exercise the vices of greed, fear, and impatience. There are countless stories of wealthy people who failed to live within their means and eventually become paupers. I devoted a chapter on protecting one's wealth in my book *"A Week to a Million Dollars; Reprogram your Mind for Wealth and Success."*

Hot on the heels of greed comes fear. If you are eager to purchase while also afraid that it will run out of stock, you will do anything within your power to purchase it because you have the capacity to. At the end of the day, we are still asking ourselves this question: Is it a necessary purchase? When you settle down in reflection, you will know that it wasn't. You could easily do without it.

Impatience is simply created by greed and fear. There is a phenomenon where people purchase something based on a promissory note. Someone promises you a certain amount of money and even before they can avail it to you, you make arrangements to buy something, mostly a want, that is commensurate to the money you are expecting. An important point to take is not spending the money you have not yet earned. Be patient enough to earn, save, invest, and then spend the proceeds of the investments.

In my legal practice, I have seen companies that have run bankrupt due to the directors' bad habits of spending funds beyond the means of the company. I have also seen couples divorce due to one party choosing to leave beyond their means. The company and the marriage could have been saved by the players simply understanding the essence of spending within their means.

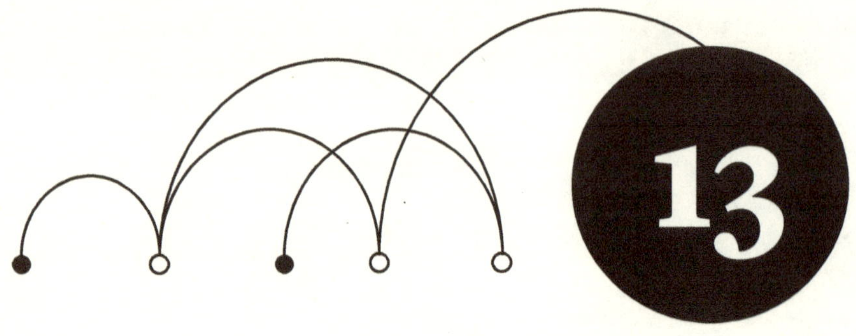

Habit 13: Avoiding Wastage

I once took stock of some of the things that we did at the office and realized that there was so much wastage of time and resources. Our bills for printing were over the roof. Before we attended meetings, the secretary would print the minutes and circulate to everyone's desk. The proposed changes would be made and then she would reprint the final copy for the meetings.

The cycle of meetings and minutes and printing continued unabated until I realized that minutes can be sent electronically, and changes done therein. How much paper could we have wasted in 50 years?

People waste a lot of time on unnecessary meetings. Some companies go an extra mile of hiring conference rooms outside of the office just to have a meeting. It is absolute wastage of time and resources, especially with the availability of free online meetings technology.

Why we should not waste?

The reason why this must be a habit is because we have to be intentional about maximization of resource use to avoid losses. When you live in a war-torn country, you will understand this without any debate. When you live in a drought or famine prone region, you will understand why every droplet of water or ounce of food counts.

We easily waste things because of the paradox of abundance. We have water flowing in our taps and that's why we at times leave the taps running. It doesn't need to take a wake-up call to jostle us into the habit of maximization. We can get conscious about it today.

Maximization as a habit is the ultimate utilization of time and resources for effectiveness and efficiency in life.

Things we waste

Time: It is a precious resource, without which other resources are difficult to come by. However, we corporately and individually waste quite a bit of time on things that don't matter. Every time we waste time, we are concurrently also wasting other resources.

At times, even the well-intended actions we take could be wastage because there could be a better alternative in their place. However, when we set out to prepare timetables, we put all the options and priorities in perspective so that we can maximize resources, time, and events.

Money: One of the biggest avenues where money is wasted, is in lifestyle. This often happens because we have not learnt the habit of self-belief and self-discipline. It is wise that you spend on only what is necessary and needed.

Food: According to the Food and Agricultural Organization, the global volume of food wastage is estimated at 1.6 billion tons. This wastage represents nearly a third of all food produced each year. The direct economic consequences of food wastage. (Excluding fish and seafood) run to the tune of $750 billion annually.

We normally waste food when we buy more than we need. Such foods get rotten in our refrigerators and is thrown away. How much food do you waste every day?

Water: It is said that the average person unknowingly wastes about 30 gallons of water daily. Water wastage occurs when we take a long-time showering, brush our teeth with a running tap, use a lot of water when washing clothes and dishes, not fix broken pipes or over filling bathtubs. This wastage can be minimised by being conscious about the monetary and environmental cost of water wastage.

Energy: Like water we many times unconsciously waste energy by forgetting to turn lights off, leaving electrical appliances on, or using outdated and energy-inefficient gadgets.

We need to eliminate wastage in our lives so as to become successful, prosperous, and fruitful in our endeavors.

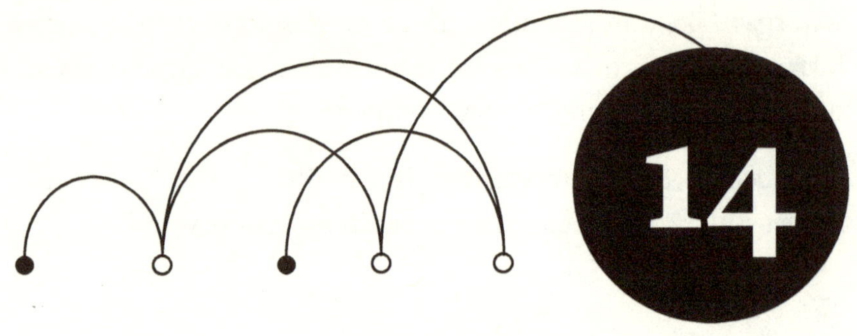

Habit 14: Consistency

What do you reckon is the most powerful thing on earth? It would be something that can never be destroyed. Is it technology? Military hardware? Science? Empires? All these things are as powerful as they can be consistent over time. Therefore, the most powerful things are those that are consistent.

By the same token, one of the most powerful habits you can ever have is consistency. Dwayne Johnson said it best:

"Success isn't always about greatness. It's about consistency. Consistent hard work leads to success. Greatness will come."

You cannot be honest, hardworking, and punctual today and behave the exact opposite tomorrow. This inconsistency will make people reluctant to trust and transact with you.

The author of Atomic Habits, James Clear, says, *"I accumulated small but consistent habits that ultimately led to results that were unimaginable when I started."*

There is a whole world to learn about consistency from these two quotes.

The result of inconsistency is confusion, lack of authenticity, and distrust among other things. It is widely quoted that Thomas Jefferson said, *'On matters of style, swim with the current, on matters of principle, stand like a rock!'* This calls for knowing when to be flexible and when to be firm and consistent.

In his book, *The Compound Effect*, Darren Hardy succinctly points out the power of small habits multiplied over time. He has a formula curated toward that effect:

Small, Smart Choices + Consistency + Time = Radical Difference

Consistency fosters reliability; an essential component for success of companies and individuals.

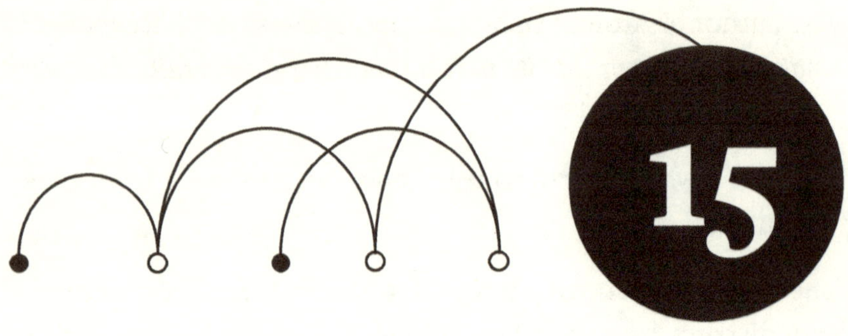

Habit 15: Hard Work

There is an age-old debate pitting hard work against "smart work." If you went to an interview and told the panel that you are lazy, there is a good chance that they will never hire you. In fact, if you asked the business owners about how they built their enterprise, they would tell you that they did not do it lazily.

The majority of successful people throughout the world and in different niches not only espouse hard work, but also preach it. If you talked to Lionel Messi or Cristiano Ronaldo, they will tell you that they are successful because of consistent practice.

Yes, they are talented and gifted in football, but as John C. Maxwell says in the book, Talent is Not Enough (Beyond Talent), *"hard work is one of those ingredients that is needed to make the complete circle of success."*

If you are habitually lazy and hate the idea of hard work, then you would look for as many excuses as you can get so that you do not work. Working "smart" can be one of those excuses, but here is the litmus test: Would you say the same thing about working smart if what you are building is your own business?

I realized that once you have clarity on what you want to achieve and why you are taking particular actions, you will not feel the "hard" in your work. You will have an inspired self-drive to achieve your goals and there is no need for anyone or anything to push you.

Hard work is not excessive toil but the devotion of a significant amount of time to accomplish a worthy cause. Morten Hansen in an article for Thrive Global on the 20th of June 2018. Defined working smart as: *To maximize the value of work by selecting a few activities and applying intense targeted effort.*

There you have it. Working Smart is not necessarily the opposite of "working hard." It is part and parcel of working hard. In other words, you are not excused from "applying intense targeted effort" to your work because you have decided to work smart! You are only working hard "in the light" and not in the dark. In other words, you are more effective and even more efficient, but you are still working hard.

Working smart also does not mean that you diminish the effort and the time you put into your work. Rather it should be concentrating skills and effort on a particular task using the most efficient methods including leveraging technology.

Working hard should lead to many benefits such as timeliness, excellence, innovativeness, teamwork and collaboration, fruitfulness, and productivity.

We need to build a work ethic so strong that we can be counted on. If you are given something to do, or if you find something to do, you apply intense force to it so much so that you do not need to be followed up or supervised. Nobody needs to micromanage you to do it. You respect yourself and your assignments so much so that it shows in the good quality of the results.

There are extremes to these facets of work. For instance, Arianna Huffington once called out Elon Musk for telling the world that on his birthday, he spent over 20 hours working. Obviously, this is detrimental to health. Working hard doesn't mean killing yourself in the process.

Death through overwork is not a myth. The phenomenon where people work themselves to death is well known in Japan and is called Karoshi. There will be seasons when you will need to do these extremes but that shouldn't be the norm.

That said, we need to look at ways in which we can both exemplify hard work as well as smart work. If you talk to business founders, you will realize that as their organizations develop, they gravitate more towards working smart than working hard, but still apply intense efforts in what they do. When you are starting out, you will be a jack of all trades. You will write the code, sell the product, market it, write articles about it, do social media posts, and all that.

This is important especially if there are no funds to pay people to do it at the start. At some point, I have been the CEO, marketing manager, accountant, and operations manager in some of my young companies. This style of working should not continue forever.

Once value starts coming in and being paid for, you have to release some tasks so that you can focus on your core roles as a business owner. Even if you are doing that, you still will work as hard as just anybody else. The following are some of the things you can do in order to integrate working hard and working smart.

Delegate: An American president who originated from Hollywood was once asked why "his economy" was thriving. He was a movies person, not an economist. He had been made fun of, and his presidency was expected to be a non-starter. It turned out that he did a stellar job so much so that people today still remember Ronald Reagan.

When asked what his secret was, he said, 'I hire my weaknesses.' That's what delegation is all about. You cannot do everything. You are not good at everything.

Hiring your weakness is getting people who are better than you to do what you can't do well so that you are released to do your core work.

Pareto Principle: Morten Hansen has already told us that working smart is about "selecting a few activities". You do not need to do all the available things. At the end of the day, the Pareto Principle tells us in effect that only a few activities done well will yield more than 80% of the results we are looking for. We need to focus on those things.

We major in the "few" things, not "small" things really, and go hard at them. It is up to you to find out what those few 20% activities in your "work" result in the most effective and productive outcome of your work. Once you have done that, you find the best way to do this, and don't spare effort, spirit, soul, and body in executing it.

Work in your passion: It is easier to work hard in what you love. Have you ever seen world-class performers complaining about working hard? In fact, Mohammad Ali is quoted to have said,

'I hated every minute of training, but I said, don't quit. Suffer now and live the rest of your life as a champion.'

It tells us that work worth doing will need sacrifice. If you hate it and are not passionate about it, when it comes to making the sacrifice, you will find an excuse or a way out.

I am convinced that working hard is a great habit that we need to cultivate. It is supposed to be in our daily disposition. I find one thing every day to work on so well and hard that when I retire to sleep, I am so fulfilled that I look forward to the next day, the next month, and the next year.

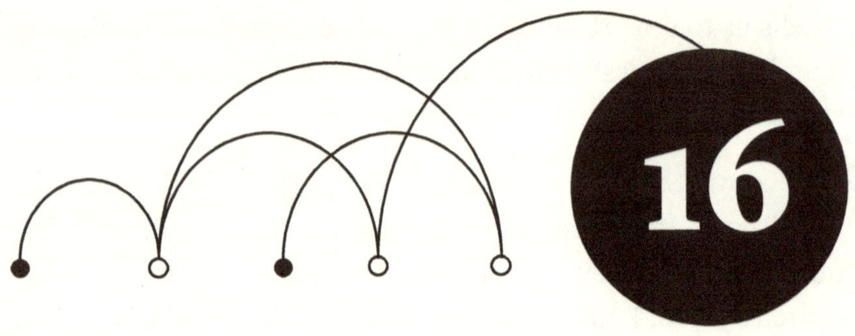

Habit 16: Being Proactive

Being proactive a is self-initiated conduct that aims to address a problem before it arises. Instead of responding to a problem as it appears, proactive behavior entails taking action in advance. Instead of accommodating a circumstance or waiting for things to happen, it refers to taking charge of a situation and making quick adjustments.

Reactivity is when you follow another person's or event's lead instead of taking the initiative to deal with a problem in your way. So, if you want to reach your goals and make your dreams come true, you need to develop the skill of being proactive.

We all likely have aspirations and objectives. But what makes us successful in life is not what we want; what we choose to do about it is what truly matters. Therefore, being proactive is crucial if you want to achieve remarkable achievements in life.

You won't ever leave your comfort zone if you are someone who always waits for things to come to you. You'll never go above and beyond. You won't ever make plans or consider your future. Instead, proactive people don't wait for opportunities to present themselves. They go out and make things to happen.

Why is proactive essential for success?

The first-mover advantage

You gain what is referred to as the first-mover advantage by being proactive. A first mover is a service or product that acquires a competitive advantage by being the first to market with a product or service. This usually allows you to build a strong brand identity and client base before rivals enter the market.

Consider Amazon. Amazon founded the first ever global e-bookstore, and it benefited by being the first to move. By the time rivals entered the market, Amazon had grown famous and had a sizable market share. Jeff Bezos probably never would have founded Amazon if he were a reactive person. He would have been of the "Let us first study the trends" school of thought, and by the time he wanted to begin, it would probably be too late.

Being proactive is crucial, especially if you are an entrepreneur. You may not make much progress if you don't take the initiative.

You'll develop a focus on the future

Future-focused folks are proactive. They consider issues from more than simply a short-term perspective and act and think in terms of their future.

Consider this: if you are only interested in the immediate payoff, you will never refuse short-term gratification. You will probably go shopping over the weekend with the extra cash when you get a raise.

Proactive individuals, however, are unique. They consider the future, and they are focused on the future. They will plan how to invest and increase their net worth after receiving a raise. They would invest the money or use it to grow their business rather than spend it all on shopping.

Because of this, proactive individuals succeed more than reactive ones. Reactive people prioritize immediate pleasure, concentrate on the immediate situation, and don't consider the future in great detail.

However, proactive individuals adopt a different perspective. They think about the future before making decisions in the present, so they can make the future they want.

You get exposed to better opportunities

Do you know that those who are proactive will have more opportunities than those who are reactive? It makes sense. Proactive people are constantly moving, and they take the initiative. As a result, they advance more and better. Along the way, they will also have chances that will help them grow and lead to better results.

Therefore, stop whining. It's not that you don't have the chance or that the timing is terrible; you need to be more aggressive, and you must be the one to take the initiative and make things happen.

You will meet more people the more you act; thus, more possibilities will present themselves to you.

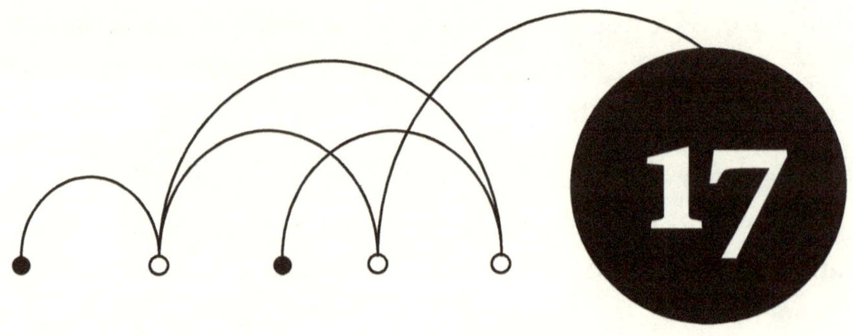

Habit 17: Staying Healthy

I once purchased cement from a hardware store and noticed that the six young men offloading a ten thousand tone trailer of cement were without any protective gear. The men placed each bag weighting about 50 Kgs on their bare backs. They ferried these for about 60 meters into the store. I counted about one ninety bags carried by the six men in the two hours I was at the store.

The day had just begun yet this was to continue throughout the day. The three of the men had stooped backs as a mark for longer service to this job of carrying heavy loads. What will happen to these young men at age 40?

The average person will spend a lot of time working in a hazardous environment only to spend all the money they have earned on medical expenses in years to come. It is a sad vicious circle.

Another common scourge affecting our generation is of non-communicable diseases. According to the World Health Organization (WHO); Non-communicable diseases kill 41 million people each year, an equivalent of 71% of all deaths globally. Each year, more than 15 million people die from an NCD between the ages of 30 and 69 years; 85% of these "premature" deaths occur in low and middle-income countries.

This information is staggering and even scary. By the time you talk about deaths to the tune of millions each year, you have not even ventured to talk about the lack of productivity that is brought about by poor health.

Diet and Nutrition

A famous quote is attributed to Hippocrates about food and medicine: *'Let medicine by your food and your food your medicine.'*

Food is therefore a critical input in our lives, whether we like it or not. It is one of the basic needs. If you remove food from a human being, you have killed him. However, over the years, we have moved away from eating for sustenance to eating for pleasure. There have been very many diseases that can be traced to wrong diet.

In fact, world-famed Dr. Don Colbert, a certified medical doctor, and author of such books as *I can Do this Diet, and The Seven Pillars of Health, says that we at times dig our graves with our spoons and knives.*

Eating a balanced diet is something we have to intentionally do and create a habit about it.

Health Exercise: In our world where entertainment and education have all converged on screens, it is possible that we exercise less than any other generation before us. Lack of exercise is toxic. The importance of exercise to the body and the brain cannot be overemphasized. Energy is always generated when we exercise, keeping us fit so that we cannot only be productive each day, but can also live longer and fight some ailments.

— PART 4 —

People Habits

It said that Fredrick II, Holy Roman Emperor conducted a diabolical experiment in the 13th century with a view of discovering which languages we are naturally born to speak. The King, a language enthusiast and a scientist of sorts took away newborn babies from their parents and placed them in the care of nurses with instructions that they should not speak to the children or within earshot of the children. He also ordered the nurses not to touch the children. The babies died.

This is called Fedrick's experiment or Language deprivation experiments or the Forbidden experiment. Fredrick's experiment shows that human beings are dependent on each other and that we need "the human touch" to survive. This is why I have considered people habits to be important and I have dedicated an entire chapter to it.

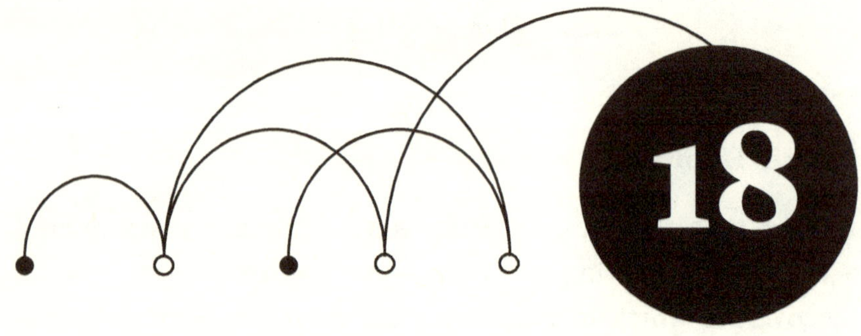

Habit 18: Courtesy

A friend of mine, employed by one of the biggest banks on the continent, was given an assignment to call up hundreds of customers and obtain information about their bank accounts. She noticed that over 95% of individuals with a lot of money in their bank accounts were courteous when she spoke to them, while those with little money in their accounts were very rude when asked the same questions.

I also read the story of a man called John Boyd. He built courtesy as one of his life philosophies. He got a job in the House of Representatives in the United States where he once observed something that was against his values. A gentleman approached a doorman asking to locate a senator from California.

The doorman kind of brushed this gentleman aside as if he didn't matter. He didn't show him courtesy. Boyd rose up and went after the gentleman and offered to find the senator he was looking for. The gentleman was so moved and gave Boyd his card, asking him to give him a call. Boyd was shocked that this gentleman was the business mogul, C. P. Huntington, the railman. The long and short of it is that Huntington offered Boyd a job in his company.

When Boyd protested that he didn't know much about the railroad, Huntington said, 'But you know how to be a gentleman, and that's what many here are ignorant of.' Boyd's salary was doubled and a year later, tripled.

Man is a social animal. We thrive in a social environment. The author of *The 7Cs in Consulting*, Mick Cope has great insights about people. In his book he writes that: "Trade is a social act" and "Organizational transformation is a people issue". I couldn't agree more. This means that even in large companies or organizations, the most important resource is not the complex machines. It is the people. Thriving in life is predicated on the number and strength of our connections to each other.

A human being who is alone and has given up can have their whole life revamped if they just get a positive connection with another human being.

Courtesy is simply showing politeness in one's interaction with others. It is an attitude that makes you consider others kindly and make them feel important and needed. The aura that courtesy creates is so powerful that it can change an environment and impact lives.

In all our relationships, where there is courtesy, there is hope that the relationship will grow stronger. It is quite important that we form the habit of courtesy to foster development and success.

You cannot attract people in your life and keep them in your circles if you lack courtesy. At best, people will stay around you because you wield some power and authority over them. However, stripped of that power and lacking courtesy, no human being will wish to stay around you. Where there is courtesy, there is respect. The two go hand in hand.

It is a life skill that can be learned. The habit of courtesy, therefore, is not something that develops by itself. Just like all the habits discussed, courtesy is built through intentional choice.

At the end of the day, you find that the benefits of showing courtesy to others are not just for them, but for you too. You certainly feel better about yourself when you are courteous to others.

Building Courtesy

Evaluate yourself: Once you get intentional about this, the first step to do is to find out how you are doing on your "courtesy index". At some level, you can know in general terms whether you are a courteous person or not. Looking at how we have treated others previously will reveal how we are doing.

Either we are courteous, mild, or totally opposite of it. It is easy to know. You have received feedback from people so far. Every time a fellow human being tells you that you were rude to them, examine your behavior to find out if it is true

Ask for feedback: It is easy to be conceited and subjective when it comes to evaluating yourself. Even when you look back at the feedback you have received from other people, it is easy to explain it away. In this step, however, you intentionally set out to get feedback from the people that you have interacted with. You want to know how you have made them feel in life. It is essential that you ask these people that you are getting feedback from to be as truthful as possible.

Set an intention and start: After you have your evaluation done, it is time to be intentional about courtesy. Start by enlisting all the things that you wish to inculcate in yourself.

Look at the following keywords and set out to show at least one to a person each day.

Benevolence	Favor	Grace
Kindness	Mercy	Service
Attention	Civility	Decorum
Etiquette	Gentleness	Politeness
Humility	Hospitality	Deference
Consideration	Thoughtfulness	Decency

Figure 7: Table of some courtesy traits

Review: Periodically review your performance. See if you are improving or not. This review will help you to firm up the habit of courtesy in your life as you move along.

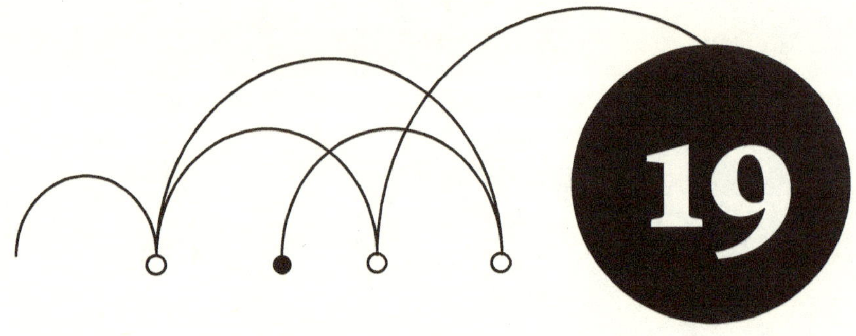

Habit 19: Respect

The summary of people habits is simply due to consideration of other beings. Growing up, we all tend to have a high regard for ourselves at the expense of other people. Nobody needs to teach us to fend for ourselves. We do it ever so naturally. It is inherent in all of us. However, consideration of others is a habit we need to learn and practice intentionally.

Respect as a habit deems that we should strive to be the ones giving it to others. We shouldn't walk around the earth demanding to be respected by others rather it is gained towards you as you give it. Some people demand to be respected because of their titles, their positions of authority, and their status in society- this is not sustainable.

What we need to learn, and this is the high road of life, is to have the habit to respect all humans regardless of whether they have material things or not.

In his book, *Leaders Eat Last*, Simon Sinek tells the story of one Stanley O'Neal, who rose to become the CEO of Merril Lynch. In Chapter 18 of that famous book, Simon explains the rise and fall of Mr. O'Neal. I can summarize it in one line: O'Neal had little respect for people but paid more attention to performance and numbers.

It is said that O'Neal had his own private elevator and instructed his managers to make sure that no employee talked to him even when they met in the corridors. He elevated himself above everyone else.

He demanded all the respect he could get. Grudgingly, people gave him what he wanted but at the expense of trust. The work environment was tainted by a leader who did not value and respect other people.

In October 2007, the company announced it had lost over $2.2 billion in the third quarter and written off $8.8 billion in failed investments. Finally, O'Neal's reign had come to an abrupt and inglorious end.

He had managed to isolate himself from his employees and his board. Ultimately, he failed miserably. It always happens that way in the end for people with on respect for others.

The interesting thing about respect or lack of it thereof is that you cannot easily quantify the advantages of giving it or the disadvantages of withholding it. The impact might not be immediate, but it is always there. The attitude of disrespect will definitely spill over to your work and business transactions and affect your productivity and results. In the end, you will lose out.

Cultivating Respect

Give automatically: As long as someone is a human being, regardless of age, race, gender, status, or color, show them respect and give them deference. Don't judge by appearances. Just give the respect that is due to the human being. In order to do this, your attitude toward all humans should be that of respect. Follow up that attitude with actions of respect. Crown the actions with words of respect. This three-cord strand of respect: Attitude, Words, and Action, will be what will help you to develop the habit.

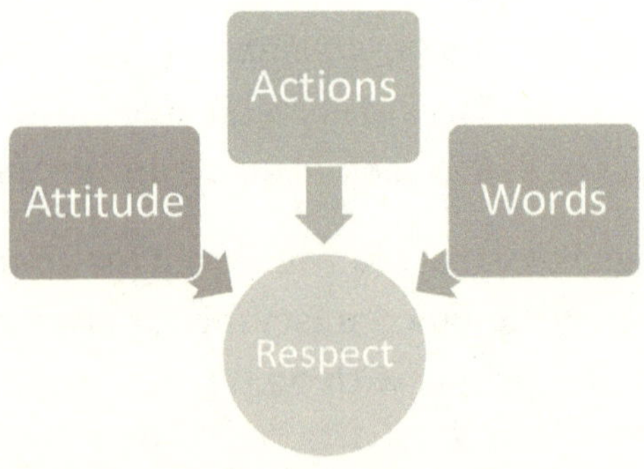

Figure 8: The three-cord strand of respect

Engage with the respectful: At some point in time, the people that you have shown respect will have to earn it going forward in a relationship. Your engagement with people in life either to do business or to have a relationship should not be blinded by the fact that they are human beings. If you deal with respectable and respectful people, your circle of respect increases. This means that not everyone should have access to your life, including the disrespectful.

Arm's length with the disrespectful: You are not obligated to live life with disrespectful people, especially those who do not want to change. In fact, your brand and reputation can easily be soiled because of such an association.

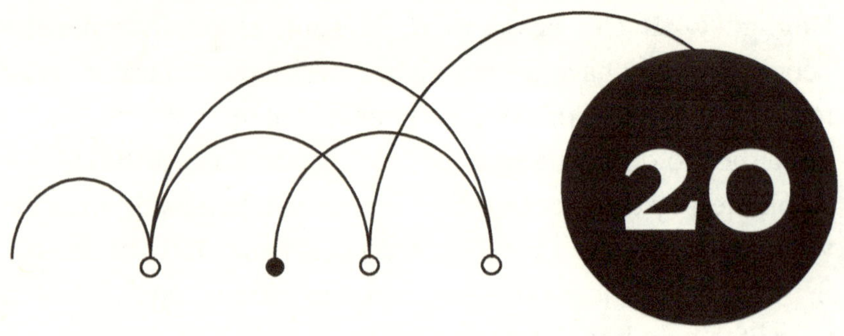

Habit 20: Mindfulness and community service

Near Lincoln, Kansas, stands a group of gravestones that boggles the imagination. A farmer named David, a self-made and determined man managed to amass a considerable fortune but had few friends and no relatives for whom he cared.

When his wife died, David erected an elaborate statue showing both her and himself sitting at the opposite ends of a loveseat. So pleased was he with this monument that he commissioned the sculptor to create another, this time showing him kneeling at her grave with a wreath in his hand. And that made such a fine impression upon him that he set out to erect still another tombstone depicting his wife kneeling at his future graveside with a wreath.

He even put wings on her back as she now resided in another world. So, as time passed and one idea led to another, he eventually spent over a quarter of a million dollars on monuments to his wife and himself.

David had no interest in aiding his fellowmen or benefiting his nearby town. Nor did he become a blessing to the church, for he used all of his resources on shrines to self. He died at the age of 92, a resident of the poorhouse, and his cherished stones are slowly but surely sinking into the Kansas soil, victimized by vandalism and neglect, and weathered by time.

Today, "mindfulness" is such a buzzword worldwide. In a world where we are increasingly talking about mental health and being conscious of mental illnesses, mindfulness comes to the fore a lot especially as we seek self-healing. I want to approach mindfulness from a totally different angle. To be mindful is not just about your self-awareness, it is about intentionally regarding other people's plight and positioning yourself, ever so continuously as one who contributes to their well-being rather than to their misery.

Among our relationships, we should always be mindful of and caring for other people. There are many things that we have control over in our personal spaces. The more we think about ourselves, the more we act for ourselves, and at times against others. This is not an ingredient of success. That's why we need to be intentional about thinking of others.

Curiosity: Take the initiative and seek information about the community and how you can contribute to its well-being.

Service: Offer yourself to voluntary service in your community. You need to participate in activities that will improve the well-being of the people around you and beyond, especially those vulnerable.

Sacrifice: If we must show care to our fellow humans, we will soon enough realize that it will not be something that we do in our stride. It has to cost us something. We need to sacrifice our time, finances, and talents for the sake of other humans. Perhaps one of the most positive traits of human relations is the sacrifice of a human being for the sake of others. Sacrifice means that we are preferring others' plight over our comfort and desires.

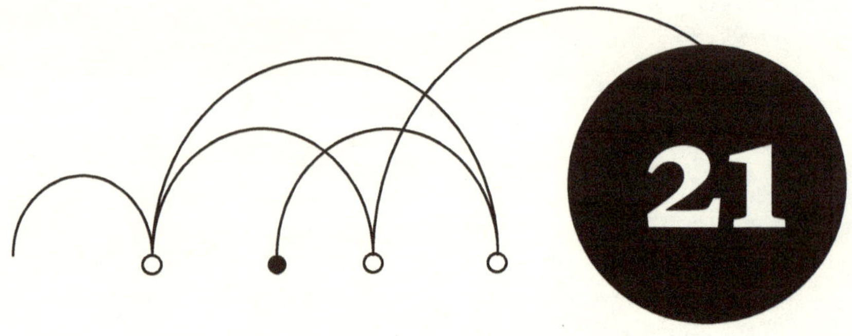

Habit 21: Keeping Good Company

The Nairobi-Kenya transport system has always intrigued the world. Articles have been written in international forums about the "Matatu Culture." A "Matatu" is a public service van that plies a particular route. It has a driver as well as a "conductor," the fellow who ushers passengers into the van and also collects the transport fare. A collection of these "Matatu" crew end up forming a sub-culture of sorts.

One day, a well-dressed young man started working as a conductor. He was totally different from the rest. In fact, he stood out. Whereas the rest mostly did not show courtesy and were not clean in their appearance and language, this young man was immaculately dressed, humble, and welcoming.

His van was always clean, and he treated everyone with the utmost respect and consideration. But this was just one young man, one strand of light amongst many. Definitely, he couldn't stand out for long.

Soon enough, he started to compromise his values so that he could fit in with the rest of the crew. The more he kept company with them, the more he accepted their way of living and doing life.

He started drinking alcohol just like the others did. He shed his immaculate appearance to fit in — in fact, he started to stand out. He drank more alcohol than they did and became even more coarse than they were. His frame started shrinking as he lost weight. In less than a year, he was no more. He died from heavy drinking.

We are admonished in scripture: Do not be deceived, bad company corrupts good morals.

We are shaped by our environment. We are also shaped, either consciously or unconsciously, by the people, we relate with. Keeping good company is an intentional thing. You intentionally allow people in your life with whom you share your values, intellect, and dreams. The more you keep company with your selection, the more your life is shaped. Jim Rohn is famed to have said the following:

'You are the average of the five people you keep company with.'

If you converse with people who are always talking about big projects that they are engaged in, you will, soon or later, start measuring up with them. Your language will change, and your outlook on life will also change.

For this habit to work, you need to define what you want out of this life. That's why we have already gone through the spirit/being habits as well as the mind habits. These will give you clarity about who you are, where you are going in this life, and why that is the case. After this is clear, it becomes abundantly easy to note that the company you keep will either build or destroy your dreams. You are the deciding factor — not the company.

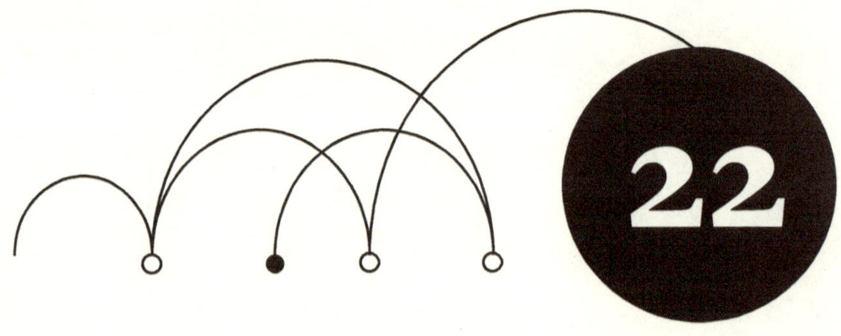

Habit 22: Forming Great Partnerships

'Two are better than one because they have a good reward for their labor. For if they fail, one will lift up his companion.' – Ecclesiastes 4:9

The importance of partnerships in life can never be overstated. Without connection and communication, it is not possible to sustain the human race. We thrive, based on our connections and networks. Our networks are indeed our net worth.

Partnerships are essentially transactional and mutual human agreements that accelerate a cause that would otherwise not fly with one person doing it alone. If you have a big vision worth its salt, you may not accomplish it alone.

It is said that it is better to have a one percent stake in a billion-dollar company than have one hundred percent ownership of a company with so much potential but with an obscure valuation because you do not want to partner with others.

Steve Jobs was with Steve Wozniak and Mark Markulla initially. Wozniak was the engineering brain, and Markulla was the financier. The three came together and formed Apple Inc. which is one of the most valuable companies in the world.

The easiest route to make no mark in this life, and have no impact is to have no partnerships at all. Look around your life today and do a personal introspection. Are there people that you can really call "partners?" Is your relationship contractual and written down? Are you contributing towards the partnership? If your answer to all of these questions is a "no," you are in danger of living below your potential and not fulfilling your destiny.

Proctor and Gamble is a multinational company that employs over 1,000 people and has a market cap of over two hundred billion dollars. Yet, in the 1830s before it was started, they were competing interests. Procter was a candle maker and Gamble was a soap maker. They were both competing for the same raw materials — animal fat and oil. It took the insight and wisdom of their father-in-law to ask them to merge their operations, and thus Procter and Gamble was formed in 1837.

The rest, as they say, is history. Think of how obscure these two relatives could have been if they had remained on course with their individual operations.

Unless we start looking past our own small inputs and ventures and start thinking of partnerships, we cannot make a great impact in the world today. Steve Jobs said, *'Great things in business are never done by one person. They are done by a team.'*

Getting partners

You need to have a specific criterion that you use as you build the habit of creating partnerships. All great partnerships had a good fit that was predicated on the quality of the individual partners. As you look for these traits in your partners, you also should have the same at varying degrees. When forming partnerships, look for the following:

Partner values: A partner whose worldview and values clash with yours is always not the right choice to do business with. For instance, if you value integrity and your partner doesn't, soon enough you will be at loggerheads when you hit crossroads. If partners do not share the same values, there will always be disagreements and conflicts in the relationship.

Partner value: This speaks of what they are bringing that is contributing to the cause that you are both pursuing. It varies from one person to the next. The worst you can get in a partner is one who contributes nothing. Partnerships are based on adding value to a cause.

If someone doesn't have obvious value addition to your cause, they cannot be your partner. If someone is highly gifted and talented in something else that is not needed in your cause, they cannot be the right fit.

Whereas some partners bring in skills and talent, others, bring money and networks.

Partner passion: The potential partner must have passion for the cause you are going to be engaged in. It is this passion that will sustain the venture afloat once hard times and uncertainty come in.

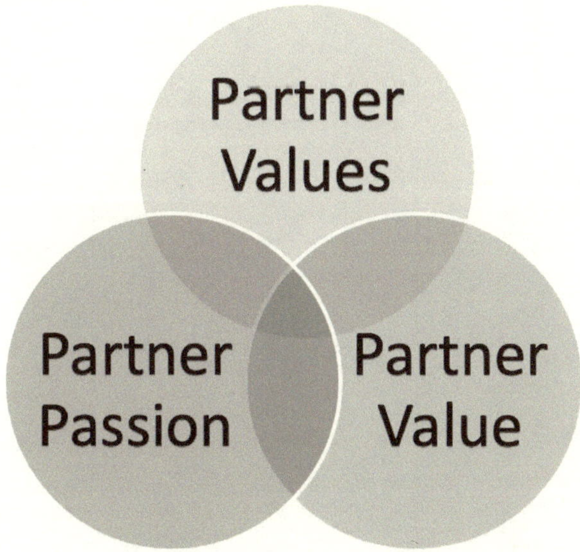

Figure 9: Qualities of partners

www.ingramcontent.com/pod-product-compliance
Lightning Source LLC
LaVergne TN
LVHW041105150826
845673LV00007B/1941